WHY TRACK Y

We all want to lead more fulfilling li~~~~~~~~~~~~, improve our outlook, and live positively. With mood tracking, all of that becomes so much simpler. When you start actively understanding the invisible parts of yourself—your emotions—you'll equip yourself with the tools to make visible changes in your day-to-day life. No one is perfectly happy all the time, but you can regain control and take steps toward a healthier, happier you!

HOW DOES IT WORK?

TRACK: As you start noting your moods throughout the week, you'll notice your emotions fluctuate. This is completely normal!

UNDERSTAND: Finding patterns in your emotions and activities will show you exactly what makes you happy, anxious, or sad.

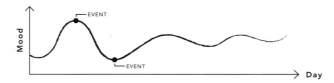

THRIVE: When you unlock this knowledge, you can choose more positive, healthier experiences. Whether that's making more time for sleep or cutting down a stressful commute, the goal isn't to be happy all the time, but to cultivate your best, balanced self.

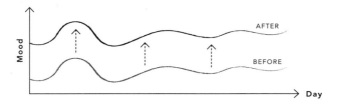

*Discover new things about yourself, stay organized
and productive, and live your best life!*

HOW TO USE YOUR MOOD TRACKER

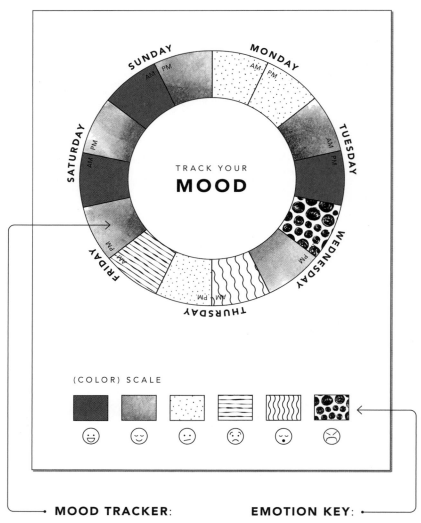

MOOD TRACKER:
Log your daily moods

EMOTION KEY:
Code your emotions
and watch how the
week takes shape

HOW TO USE YOUR MOOD TRACKER

REFLECT ON YOUR MOODS THIS WEEK.

Happy/excited ~ saw a lot of people I love, and I felt energized and well-rested.

WHAT IMPACTED YOUR MOOD?

POSITIVE	NEUTRAL	NEGATIVE
Saw BFF	Regular work	Got a flat tire
Got lots of sleep	routine	and late for work

REFLECT ON YOUR MOODS:

Reflect on your tracker and the effects of your week's activities

WHAT IMPACTED YOUR MOOD:

Evaluate positive and negative experiences

HOW TO USE YOUR MONTHLY GOAL TRACKER

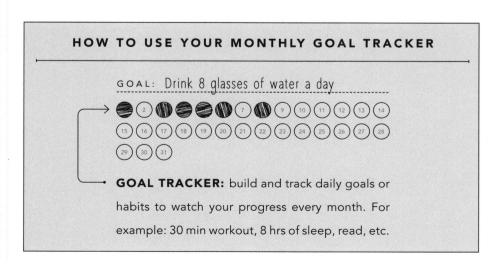

GOAL: Drink 8 glasses of water a day

GOAL TRACKER: build and track daily goals or habits to watch your progress every month. For example: 30 min workout, 8 hrs of sleep, read, etc.

JANUARY

MONDAY	TUESDAY	WEDNESDAY	THURSDAY	FRIDAY
2 *Day after New Year's Day (NZ, SCT)*	3	4	5	6
9	10	11	12	13
16 *Martin Luther King Jr. Day*	17	18	19	20
23	24	25	26	27
30	31		*Australia Day (AUS)*	

02

03

04

05/06

SATURDAY	SUNDAY
	1
	New Year's Day
7	8
14	15
21	22
	Chinese New Year
28	29

01 02 03 04 05

NOTES

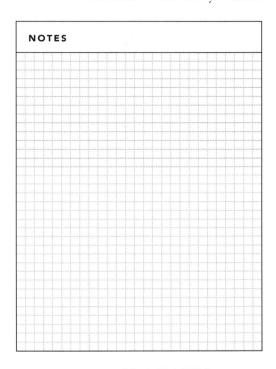

MONTHLY GOAL TRACKER

GOAL: -------------------------------------

1 2 3 4 5 6 7 8 9 10 11 12 13 14
15 16 17 18 19 20 21 22 23 24 25 26 27 28
29 30 31

GOAL: -------------------------------------

1 2 3 4 5 6 7 8 9 10 11 12 13 14
15 16 17 18 19 20 21 22 23 24 25 26 27 28
29 30 31

GOAL: -------------------------------------

1 2 3 4 5 6 7 8 9 10 11 12 13 14
15 16 17 18 19 20 21 22 23 24 25 26 27 28
29 30 31

WEEKLY GOALS

1 ----------------------------------

----

2 ----------------------------------

----

3 ----------------------------------

TO DO

- • ----------------------------------
- • ----------------------------------
- • ----------------------------------
- • ----------------------------------
- • ----------------------------------
- • ----------------------------------
- • ----------------------------------
- • ----------------------------------
- • ----------------------------------
- • ----------------------------------

After all, tomorrow is another day!

—MARGARET MITCHELL, *GONE WITH THE WIND*

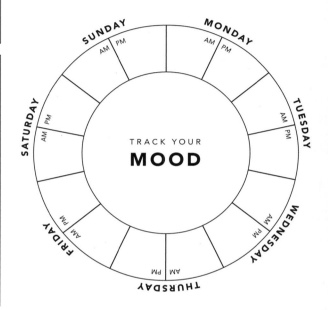

DECEMBER 2022

Mo	Tu	We	Th	Fr	Sa	Su
			1	2	3	4
5	6	7	8	9	10	11
12	13	14	15	16	17	18
19	20	21	22	23	24	25
26	27	28	29	30	31	

FEBRUARY 2023

Mo	Tu	We	Th	Fr	Sa	Su
		1	2	3	4	5
6	7	8	9	10	11	12
13	14	15	16	17	18	19
20	21	22	23	24	25	26
27	28					

(COLOR) SCALE

NOTES

DECEMBER/JANUARY

26 **MONDAY** *Kwanzaa begins*
Boxing Day (AUS, CAN, NZ, UK)

27 **TUESDAY**

28 **WEDNESDAY**

29 **THURSDAY**

30 **FRIDAY**

31 **SATURDAY** *New Year's Eve*

1 **SUNDAY** *New Year's Day*

REFLECT ON YOUR MOODS THIS WEEK.

WHAT IMPACTED YOUR MOOD?

POSITIVE	NEUTRAL	NEGATIVE

WRITE ABOUT YOUR FAVORITE MEMORY FROM LAST YEAR. HOW CAN YOU INCORPORATE ANOTHER EXPERIENCE LIKE THAT INTO 2023?

THIS WEEK'S HAPPY MOMENT

THIS WEEK I'M GRATEFUL FOR

WEEKLY GOALS

1

2

3

TO DO

- --------------------------------
- --------------------------------
- --------------------------------
- --------------------------------
- --------------------------------
- --------------------------------
- --------------------------------
- --------------------------------
- --------------------------------

What day is so dark that there is no ray of sunshine to penetrate the gloom?

—MARY TODD LINCOLN

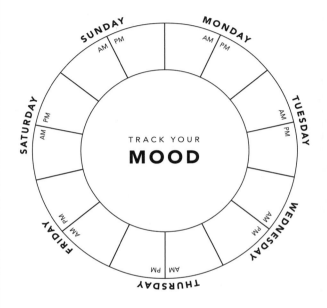

TRACK YOUR
MOOD

DECEMBER 2022

Mo	Tu	We	Th	Fr	Sa	Su
			1	2	3	4
5	6	7	8	9	10	11
12	13	14	15	16	17	18
19	20	21	22	23	24	25
26	27	28	29	30	31	

FEBRUARY 2023

Mo	Tu	We	Th	Fr	Sa	Su
		1	2	3	4	5
6	7	8	9	10	11	12
13	14	15	16	17	18	19
20	21	22	23	24	25	26
27	28					

(COLOR) SCALE

NOTES

JANUARY

2 | **MONDAY**   *Day after New Year's Day (NZ, SCT)*

3 | **TUESDAY**

4 | **WEDNESDAY**

5 | **THURSDAY**

6 | **FRIDAY**

7 | **SATURDAY**

8 | **SUNDAY**

REFLECT ON YOUR MOODS THIS WEEK.

WHAT IMPACTED YOUR MOOD?

POSITIVE	NEUTRAL	NEGATIVE

MAKE A POINT TO SPEND SOME TIME WITH YOURSELF. CREATE A LIST OF ACTIVITIES YOU HAVE WANTED TO DO FOR A WHILE, AND FIND A WAY TO ACCOMPLISH AT LEAST ONE THIS WEEK.

THIS WEEK'S HAPPY MOMENT

THIS WEEK I'M GRATEFUL FOR

WEEKLY GOALS

1 _____
_____

2 _____
_____

3 _____
_____

TO DO

• _____
• _____
• _____
• _____
• _____
• _____
• _____
• _____
• _____
• _____

Contemplation seems to be about the only luxury that costs nothing.

—DODIE SMITH

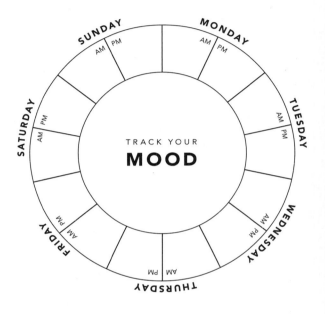

DECEMBER 2022

Mo	Tu	We	Th	Fr	Sa	Su
			1	2	3	4
5	6	7	8	9	10	11
12	13	14	15	16	17	18
19	20	21	22	23	24	25
26	27	28	29	30	31	

FEBRUARY 2023

Mo	Tu	We	Th	Fr	Sa	Su
		1	2	3	4	5
6	7	8	9	10	11	12
13	14	15	16	17	18	19
20	21	22	23	24	25	26
27	28					

(COLOR) SCALE

NOTES

JANUARY

9 | MONDAY

10 | TUESDAY

11 | WEDNESDAY

12 | THURSDAY

13 | FRIDAY

14 | SATURDAY

15 | SUNDAY

REFLECT ON YOUR MOODS THIS WEEK.

WHAT IMPACTED YOUR MOOD?

POSITIVE	NEUTRAL	NEGATIVE

WHERE DO YOU FIND THE MOST VALUE IN YOUR LIFE? IS IT IN YOUR
RELATIONSHIPS? YOUR WORK? SOMETHING ELSE?

THIS WEEK'S HAPPY MOMENT

THIS WEEK I'M GRATEFUL FOR

WEEKLY GOALS

1 ....

....

2 ....

....

3 ....

....

TO DO

- ....
- ....
- ....
- ....
- ....
- ....
- ....
- ....
- ....
- ....

Many of our fears are tissue-paper thin, and a single courageous step would carry us clear through them.

—BRENDAN FRANCIS BEHAN

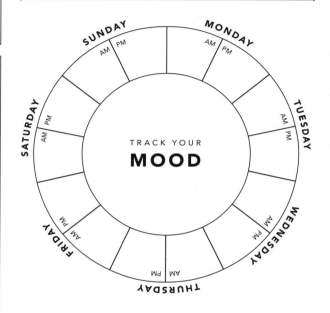

TRACK YOUR
MOOD

DECEMBER 2022

Mo	Tu	We	Th	Fr	Sa	Su
			1	2	3	4
5	6	7	8	9	10	11
12	13	14	15	16	17	18
19	20	21	22	23	24	25
26	27	28	29	30	31	

FEBRUARY 2023

Mo	Tu	We	Th	Fr	Sa	Su
		1	2	3	4	5
6	7	8	9	10	11	12
13	14	15	16	17	18	19
20	21	22	23	24	25	26
27	28					

(COLOR) SCALE

NOTES

JANUARY

16 **MONDAY** *Martin Luther King Jr. Day*

17 **TUESDAY**

18 **WEDNESDAY**

19 **THURSDAY**

20 **FRIDAY**

21 **SATURDAY**

22 **SUNDAY** *Chinese New Year*

REFLECT ON YOUR MOODS THIS WEEK.

WHAT IMPACTED YOUR MOOD?

POSITIVE	NEUTRAL	NEGATIVE

BRAINSTORM SOME WAYS TO MAKE THIS WEEK BETTER THAN LAST. WHAT CAN YOU ADD TO OR TAKE AWAY FROM YOUR ROUTINE TO CHANGE YOUR MOOD?

THIS WEEK'S HAPPY MOMENT

THIS WEEK I'M GRATEFUL FOR

WEEKLY GOALS

1

2

3

TO DO

- -----------------------------------
- -----------------------------------
- -----------------------------------
- -----------------------------------
- -----------------------------------
- -----------------------------------
- -----------------------------------
- -----------------------------------
- -----------------------------------
- -----------------------------------

To shine your brightest light is to be who you truly are.

—ROY T. BENNETT

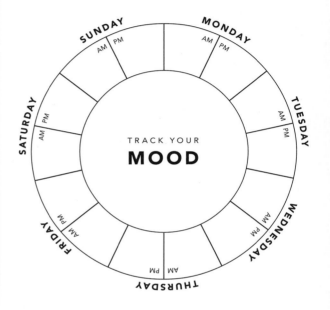

DECEMBER 2022

Mo	Tu	We	Th	Fr	Sa	Su
			1	2	3	4
5	6	7	8	9	10	11
12	13	14	15	16	17	18
19	20	21	22	23	24	25
26	27	28	29	30	31	

FEBRUARY 2023

Mo	Tu	We	Th	Fr	Sa	Su
		1	2	3	4	5
6	7	8	9	10	11	12
13	14	15	16	17	18	19
20	21	22	23	24	25	26
27	28					

(COLOR) SCALE

NOTES

JANUARY

---

23 | **MONDAY**

24 | **TUESDAY**

25 | **WEDNESDAY**

26 | **THURSDAY** *Australia Day (AUS)*

27 | **FRIDAY**

28 | **SATURDAY**

29 | **SUNDAY**

REFLECT ON YOUR MOODS THIS WEEK.

WHAT IMPACTED YOUR MOOD?

POSITIVE	NEUTRAL	NEGATIVE

MONTHLY REFLECTION: WHAT MOST AFFECTED YOUR MOOD THIS MONTH?

THIS WEEK'S HAPPY MOMENT

THIS WEEK I'M GRATEFUL FOR

FEBRUARY

MONDAY	TUESDAY	WEDNESDAY	THURSDAY	FRIDAY
		1	2	3
			Groundhog Day	
6	7	8	9	10
Waitangi Day (NZ)				
13	14	15	16	17
	Valentine's Day			
20	21	22	23	24
Presidents' Day		*Ash Wednesday (Lent begins)*		
27	28			

06
07
08
09
10

SATURDAY	SUNDAY
4	5
11	12 *Abraham Lincoln's Birthday*
18	19
25	26

06
07
08
09

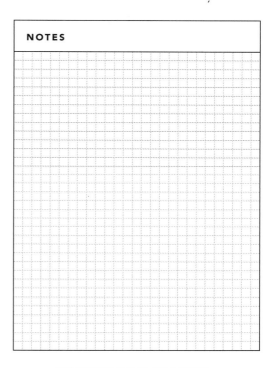

NOTES

MONTHLY GOAL TRACKER

G O A L :

① ② ③ ④ ⑤ ⑥ ⑦ ⑧ ⑨ ⑩ ⑪ ⑫ ⑬ ⑭
⑮ ⑯ ⑰ ⑱ ⑲ ⑳ ㉑ ㉒ ㉓ ㉔ ㉕ ㉖ ㉗ ㉘
㉙ ㉚ ㉛

G O A L :

① ② ③ ④ ⑤ ⑥ ⑦ ⑧ ⑨ ⑩ ⑪ ⑫ ⑬ ⑭
⑮ ⑯ ⑰ ⑱ ⑲ ⑳ ㉑ ㉒ ㉓ ㉔ ㉕ ㉖ ㉗ ㉘
㉙ ㉚ ㉛

G O A L :

① ② ③ ④ ⑤ ⑥ ⑦ ⑧ ⑨ ⑩ ⑪ ⑫ ⑬ ⑭
⑮ ⑯ ⑰ ⑱ ⑲ ⑳ ㉑ ㉒ ㉓ ㉔ ㉕ ㉖ ㉗ ㉘
㉙ ㉚ ㉛

WEEKLY GOALS

1 --------------------------------

----

2 --------------------------------

----

3 --------------------------------

TO DO

- --------------------------------
- --------------------------------
- --------------------------------
- --------------------------------
- --------------------------------
- --------------------------------
- --------------------------------
- --------------------------------
- --------------------------------
- --------------------------------

To love oneself is the beginning of a lifelong romance.

—OSCAR WILDE, *AN IDEAL HUSBAND*

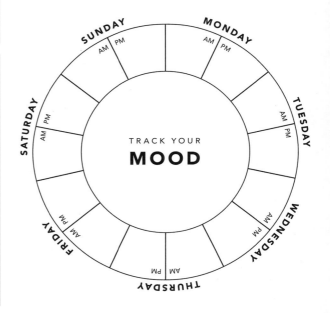

TRACK YOUR
MOOD

JANUARY 2023

Mo	Tu	We	Th	Fr	Sa	Su
						1
2	3	4	5	6	7	8
9	10	11	12	13	14	15
16	17	18	19	20	21	22
23	24	25	26	27	28	29
30	31					

MARCH 2023

Mo	Tu	We	Th	Fr	Sa	Su
		1	2	3	4	5
6	7	8	9	10	11	12
13	14	15	16	17	18	19
20	21	22	23	24	25	26
27	28	29	30	31		

(COLOR) SCALE

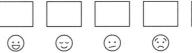

NOTES

JANUARY/FEBRUARY

30 | MONDAY

31 | TUESDAY

1 | WEDNESDAY

2 | THURSDAY   *Groundhog Day*

3 | FRIDAY

4 | SATURDAY

5 | SUNDAY

REFLECT ON YOUR MOODS THIS WEEK.

WHAT IMPACTED YOUR MOOD?

POSITIVE	NEUTRAL	NEGATIVE

IF THERE WAS ONE THING YOU COULD CHANGE IN YOUR LIFE
INSTANTANEOUSLY, WHAT WOULD THAT BE? CAN YOU CREATE A DAILY
PLAN TO START WORKING TO CHANGE THAT THING?

THIS WEEK'S HAPPY MOMENT

THIS WEEK I'M GRATEFUL FOR

WEEKLY GOALS

1

2

3

TO DO

- -------------------------------------
- -------------------------------------
- -------------------------------------
- -------------------------------------
- -------------------------------------
- -------------------------------------
- -------------------------------------
- -------------------------------------
- -------------------------------------
- -------------------------------------

That is happiness; to be dissolved into something complete and great.

—WILLA CATHER

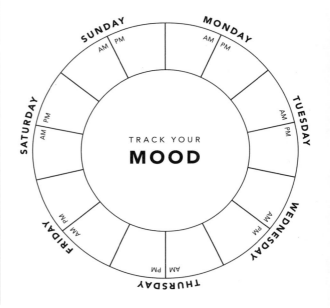

JANUARY 2023

Mo	Tu	We	Th	Fr	Sa	Su
						1
2	3	4	5	6	7	8
9	10	11	12	13	14	15
16	17	18	19	20	21	22
23	24	25	26	27	28	29
30	31					

MARCH 2023

Mo	Tu	We	Th	Fr	Sa	Su
		1	2	3	4	5
6	7	8	9	10	11	12
13	14	15	16	17	18	19
20	21	22	23	24	25	26
27	28	29	30	31		

(COLOR) SCALE

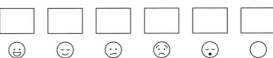

NOTES

FEBRUARY

WEEK 07 // 2023

6 MONDAY *Waitangi Day (NZ)*

7 TUESDAY

8 WEDNESDAY

9 THURSDAY

10 FRIDAY

11 SATURDAY

12 SUNDAY *Abraham Lincoln's Birthday*

REFLECT ON YOUR MOODS THIS WEEK.

WHAT IMPACTED YOUR MOOD?

POSITIVE	NEUTRAL	NEGATIVE

FEBRUARY 6—FEBRUARY 12   WEEK 07 / 2023

WHAT'S ONE MOMENT YOU WANT TO REMEMBER FROM LAST WEEK? WHY?

THIS WEEK'S HAPPY MOMENT

THIS WEEK I'M GRATEFUL FOR

WEEKLY GOALS

1 ------------------------------------
----

2 ------------------------------------
----

3 ------------------------------------

TO DO

• ------------------------------------
• ------------------------------------
• ------------------------------------
• ------------------------------------
• ------------------------------------
• ------------------------------------
• ------------------------------------
• ------------------------------------
• ------------------------------------
• ------------------------------------

I celebrate myself, and sing myself.

—WALT WHITMAN, "SONG OF MYSELF"

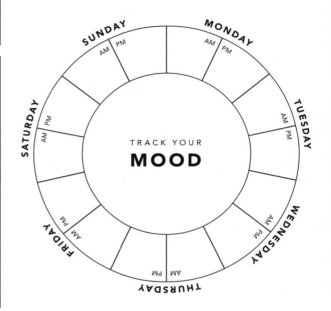

TRACK YOUR
MOOD

JANUARY 2023

Mo	Tu	We	Th	Fr	Sa	Su
						1
2	3	4	5	6	7	8
9	10	11	12	13	14	15
16	17	18	19	20	21	22
23	24	25	26	27	28	29
30	31					

MARCH 2023

Mo	Tu	We	Th	Fr	Sa	Su
		1	2	3	4	5
6	7	8	9	10	11	12
13	14	15	16	17	18	19
20	21	22	23	24	25	26
27	28	29	30	31		

(COLOR) SCALE

NOTES

FEBRUARY

13 | **MONDAY**

14 | **TUESDAY**   *Valentine's Day*

15 | **WEDNESDAY**

16 | **THURSDAY**

17 | **FRIDAY**

18 | **SATURDAY**

19 | **SUNDAY**

REFLECT ON YOUR MOODS THIS WEEK.

WHAT IMPACTED YOUR MOOD?

POSITIVE	NEUTRAL	NEGATIVE

WHAT IS AN IDEA, PRINCIPLE, OR BELIEF THAT IS IMPORTANT TO YOU?

THIS WEEK'S HAPPY MOMENT

THIS WEEK I'M GRATEFUL FOR

WEEKLY GOALS

1 ------------------------------
----

2 ------------------------------
----

3 ------------------------------

Don't turn away. Keep your gaze on the bandaged place. That's where the light enters you.

—RUMI

TO DO

- ------------------------------
- ------------------------------
- ------------------------------
- ------------------------------
- ------------------------------
- ------------------------------
- ------------------------------
- ------------------------------
- ------------------------------
- ------------------------------

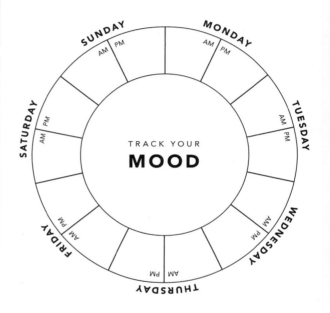

JANUARY 2023

Mo	Tu	We	Th	Fr	Sa	Su
						1
2	3	4	5	6	7	8
9	10	11	12	13	14	15
16	17	18	19	20	21	22
23	24	25	26	27	28	29
30	31					

(COLOR) SCALE

MARCH 2023

Mo	Tu	We	Th	Fr	Sa	Su
		1	2	3	4	5
6	7	8	9	10	11	12
13	14	15	16	17	18	19
20	21	22	23	24	25	26
27	28	29	30	31		

NOTES

FEBRUARY

20 | **MONDAY**   *Presidents' Day*

21 | **TUESDAY**

22 | **WEDNESDAY**   *Ash Wednesday (Lent begins)*

23 | **THURSDAY**

24 | **FRIDAY**

25 | **SATURDAY**

26 | **SUNDAY**

REFLECT ON YOUR MOODS THIS WEEK.

WHAT IMPACTED YOUR MOOD?

POSITIVE	NEUTRAL	NEGATIVE

FEBRUARY 20—FEBRUARY 26

WEEK 09 / 2023

MONTHLY REFLECTION: WHAT MOST AFFECTED YOUR MOOD THIS MONTH?

THIS WEEK'S HAPPY MOMENT

THIS WEEK I'M GRATEFUL FOR

MARCH

MONDAY	TUESDAY	WEDNESDAY	THURSDAY	FRIDAY
		1	2	3
6 *Purim begins*	7	8 *International Women's Day*	9	10
13 *Public Holiday (AUS: ACT, SA, TAS, VIC)*	14	15	16	17 *St. Patrick's Day*
20 *Spring begins (Northern Hemisphere)*	21	22 *Ramadan begins*	23	24
27	28	29	30	31

10

11

12

13

14

SATURDAY	SUNDAY
4	5
11	12
	Daylight Saving Time begins (USA, CAN)
18	19
	Mothering Sunday (UK)
25	26

10
11
12
13

NOTES

MONTHLY GOAL TRACKER

GOAL:

1 2 3 4 5 6 7 8 9 10 11 12 13 14
15 16 17 18 19 20 21 22 23 24 25 26 27 28
29 30 31

GOAL:

1 2 3 4 5 6 7 8 9 10 11 12 13 14
15 16 17 18 19 20 21 22 23 24 25 26 27 28
29 30 31

GOAL:

1 2 3 4 5 6 7 8 9 10 11 12 13 14
15 16 17 18 19 20 21 22 23 24 25 26 27 28
29 30 31

WEEKLY GOALS

1
....

2
....

3
....

....

TO DO

- ....
- ....
- ....
- ....
- ....
- ....
- ....
- ....
- ....
- ....

One must still have chaos within oneself to give birth to a dancing star.

—FRIEDRICH NIETZSCHE

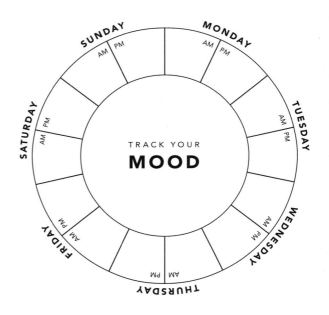

TRACK YOUR
MOOD

FEBRUARY 2023

Mo	Tu	We	Th	Fr	Sa	Su
		1	2	3	4	5
6	7	8	9	10	11	12
13	14	15	16	17	18	19
20	21	22	23	24	25	26
27	28					

APRIL 2023

Mo	Tu	We	Th	Fr	Sa	Su
					1	2
3	4	5	6	7	8	9
10	11	12	13	14	15	16
17	18	19	20	21	22	23
24	25	26	27	28	29	30

(COLOR) SCALE

NOTES

27 | MONDAY

28 | TUESDAY

1 | WEDNESDAY

2 | THURSDAY

3 | FRIDAY

4 | SATURDAY

5 | SUNDAY

REFLECT ON YOUR MOODS THIS WEEK.

WHAT IMPACTED YOUR MOOD?

POSITIVE	NEUTRAL	NEGATIVE

PLAN OUT YOUR MEALS FOR THIS UPCOMING WEEK. EATING WELL IS INCREDIBLY IMPORTANT FOR COMBATING THE PHYSICAL AND MENTAL EFFECTS OF STRESS.

THIS WEEK'S HAPPY MOMENT

THIS WEEK I'M GRATEFUL FOR

WEEKLY GOALS

1 ---------------------------------
----
2 ---------------------------------
----
3 ---------------------------------

TO DO

- • ---------------------------------
- • ---------------------------------
- • ---------------------------------
- • ---------------------------------
- • ---------------------------------
- • ---------------------------------
- • ---------------------------------
- • ---------------------------------
- • ---------------------------------
- • ---------------------------------

Don't go through life, grow through life.

—ERIC BUTTERWORTH

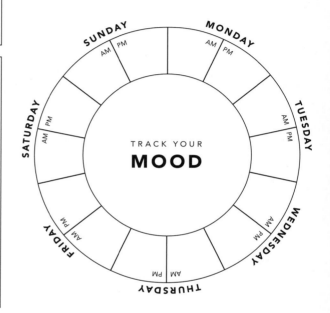

FEBRUARY 2023

Mo	Tu	We	Th	Fr	Sa	Su
		1	2	3	4	5
6	7	8	9	10	11	12
13	14	15	16	17	18	19
20	21	22	23	24	25	26
27	28					

APRIL 2023

Mo	Tu	We	Th	Fr	Sa	Su
					1	2
3	4	5	6	7	8	9
10	11	12	13	14	15	16
17	18	19	20	21	22	23
24	25	26	27	28	29	30

(COLOR) SCALE

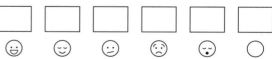

NOTES

MARCH

6 | **MONDAY**   *Purim begins*

7 | **TUESDAY**

8 | **WEDNESDAY**   *International Women's Day*

9 | **THURSDAY**

10 | **FRIDAY**

11 | **SATURDAY**

12 | **SUNDAY**   *Daylight Saving Time begins (USA, CAN)*

REFLECT ON YOUR MOODS THIS WEEK.

WHAT IMPACTED YOUR MOOD?

POSITIVE	NEUTRAL	NEGATIVE

JOT DOWN SOMETHING SMALL THAT BRINGS YOU BIG JOY. HOW CAN YOU
INCORPORATE THAT INTO YOUR DAILY LIFE MORE OFTEN?

THIS WEEK'S HAPPY MOMENT

THIS WEEK I'M GRATEFUL FOR

WEEKLY GOALS

1

2

3

TO DO

- -------------------------------------
- -------------------------------------
- -------------------------------------
- -------------------------------------
- -------------------------------------
- -------------------------------------
- -------------------------------------
- -------------------------------------
- -------------------------------------
- -------------------------------------

Most of the shadows of this life are caused by standing in one's own sunshine.

—RALPH WALDO EMERSON

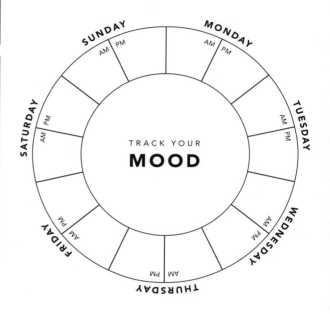

TRACK YOUR
MOOD

FEBRUARY 2023

Mo	Tu	We	Th	Fr	Sa	Su
		1	2	3	4	5
6	7	8	9	10	11	12
13	14	15	16	17	18	19
20	21	22	23	24	25	26
27	28					

APRIL 2023

Mo	Tu	We	Th	Fr	Sa	Su
					1	2
3	4	5	6	7	8	9
10	11	12	13	14	15	16
17	18	19	20	21	22	23
24	25	26	27	28	29	30

(COLOR) SCALE

NOTES

MARCH

13 **MONDAY** *Public Holiday (AUS: ACT, SA, TAS, VIC)*

14 **TUESDAY**

15 **WEDNESDAY**

16 **THURSDAY**

17 **FRIDAY** *St. Patrick's Day*

18 **SATURDAY**

19 **SUNDAY** *Mothering Sunday (UK)*

REFLECT ON YOUR MOODS THIS WEEK.

WHAT IMPACTED YOUR MOOD?

POSITIVE	NEUTRAL	NEGATIVE

SOMETIMES IT'S GOOD TO ACKNOWLEDGE THE THINGS YOU DIDN'T DO.
WHAT'S ONE HABIT OR ACTION THAT YOU HAVEN'T DONE RECENTLY THAT
YOU'RE PROUD OF?

THIS WEEK'S HAPPY MOMENT

THIS WEEK I'M GRATEFUL FOR

WEEKLY GOALS

1 ....
....

2 ....
....

3 ....
....

TO DO

- ....
- ....
- ....
- ....
- ....
- ....
- ....
- ....
- ....
- ....

Imperfections are not inadequacies; they are reminders that we're all in this together.

—BRENÉ BROWN

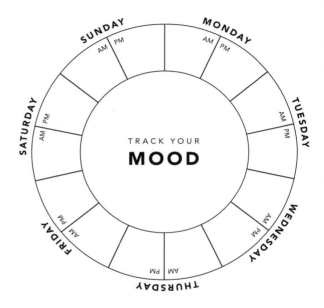

TRACK YOUR **MOOD**

FEBRUARY 2023

Mo	Tu	We	Th	Fr	Sa	Su
		1	2	3	4	5
6	7	8	9	10	11	12
13	14	15	16	17	18	19
20	21	22	23	24	25	26
27	28					

APRIL 2023

Mo	Tu	We	Th	Fr	Sa	Su
					1	2
3	4	5	6	7	8	9
10	11	12	13	14	15	16
17	18	19	20	21	22	23
24	25	26	27	28	29	30

(COLOR) SCALE

NOTES

20 | **MONDAY** *Spring Begins (Northern Hemisphere)*

21 | **TUESDAY**

22 | **WEDNESDAY** *Ramadan begins*

23 | **THURSDAY**

24 | **FRIDAY**

25 | **SATURDAY**

26 | **SUNDAY**

REFLECT ON YOUR MOODS THIS WEEK.

WHAT IMPACTED YOUR MOOD?

POSITIVE	NEUTRAL	NEGATIVE

WHAT IS YOUR BIGGEST CONCERN THIS WEEK? SPEND SOME TIME BREAKING IT DOWN INTO SMALLER ISSUES OR TASKS. HOW CAN YOU ADDRESS THOSE PIECES RATHER THAN TRY TO TACKLE THE WHOLE PROBLEM AT ONCE?

THIS WEEK'S HAPPY MOMENT

THIS WEEK I'M GRATEFUL FOR

WEEKLY GOALS

1 --
----

2 --
----

3 --

TO DO

- --
- --
- --
- --
- --
- --
- --
- --
- --
- --

> By doing the work to love ourselves more, I believe we will love each other better.
>
> —LAVERNE COX

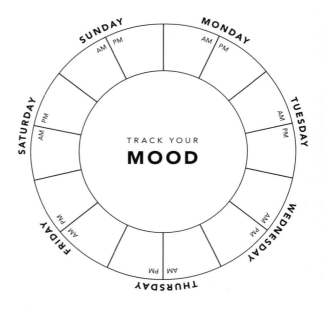

TRACK YOUR
MOOD

FEBRUARY 2023

Mo	Tu	We	Th	Fr	Sa	Su
		1	2	3	4	5
6	7	8	9	10	11	12
13	14	15	16	17	18	19
20	21	22	23	24	25	26
27	28					

APRIL 2023

Mo	Tu	We	Th	Fr	Sa	Su
					1	2
3	4	5	6	7	8	9
10	11	12	13	14	15	16
17	18	19	20	21	22	23
24	25	26	27	28	29	30

(COLOR) SCALE

MARCH/APRIL

WEEK 14 // 2023

27 | **MONDAY**

28 | **TUESDAY**

29 | **WEDNESDAY**

30 | **THURSDAY**

31 | **FRIDAY**

1 | **SATURDAY** *April Fools' Day*

2 | **SUNDAY** *Palm Sunday*

REFLECT ON YOUR MOODS THIS WEEK.

WHAT IMPACTED YOUR MOOD?

POSITIVE	NEUTRAL	NEGATIVE

MONTHLY REFLECTION: WHAT MOST AFFECTED YOUR MOOD THIS MONTH?

THIS WEEK'S HAPPY MOMENT

THIS WEEK I'M GRATEFUL FOR

APRIL

MONDAY	TUESDAY	WEDNESDAY	THURSDAY	FRIDAY
3	4	5	6	7
		Passover begins		*Good Friday*
10	11	12	13	14
Easter Monday (AUS, CAN, NZ, UK except SCT)				
17	18	19	20	21
	Tax Day			*Eid al-Fitr begins*
24	25	26	27	28
	Anzac Day (AUS, NZ)			*Workers' Memorial Day (UK)*

14

15

16

17

18

SATURDAY	SUNDAY
1	2
April Fools' Day	*Palm Sunday*
8	9
	Easter
15	16
22	23
Earth Day	
29	30

14
15
16
17
18

NOTES

MONTHLY GOAL TRACKER

GOAL:

(1) (2) (3) (4) (5) (6) (7) (8) (9) (10) (11) (12) (13) (14)
(15) (16) (17) (18) (19) (20) (21) (22) (23) (24) (25) (26) (27) (28)
(29) (30) (31)

GOAL:

(1) (2) (3) (4) (5) (6) (7) (8) (9) (10) (11) (12) (13) (14)
(15) (16) (17) (18) (19) (20) (21) (22) (23) (24) (25) (26) (27) (28)
(29) (30) (31)

GOAL:

(1) (2) (3) (4) (5) (6) (7) (8) (9) (10) (11) (12) (13) (14)
(15) (16) (17) (18) (19) (20) (21) (22) (23) (24) (25) (26) (27) (28)
(29) (30) (31)

WEEKLY GOALS

1 --
----

2 --
----

3 --

TO DO

• --
• --
• --
• --
• --
• --
• --
• --
• --
• --

If your compassion does not include yourself, it is incomplete.

—JACK KORNFIELD

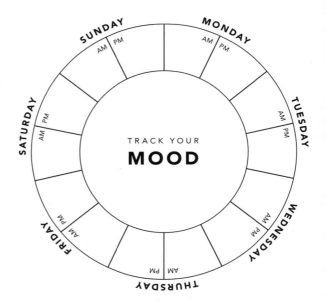

TRACK YOUR **MOOD**

MARCH 2023

Mo	Tu	We	Th	Fr	Sa	Su
		1	2	3	4	5
6	7	8	9	10	11	12
13	14	15	16	17	18	19
20	21	22	23	24	25	26
27	28	29	30	31		

MAY 2023

Mo	Tu	We	Th	Fr	Sa	Su
1	2	3	4	5	6	7
8	9	10	11	12	13	14
15	16	17	18	19	20	21
22	23	24	25	26	27	28
29	30	31				

(COLOR) SCALE

NOTES

APRIL

3 **MONDAY**

---

4 **TUESDAY**

---

5 **WEDNESDAY** *Passover begins*

---

6 **THURSDAY**

---

7 **FRIDAY** *Good Friday*

---

8 **SATURDAY**

9 **SUNDAY** *Easter*

REFLECT ON YOUR MOODS THIS WEEK.

WHAT IMPACTED YOUR MOOD?

POSITIVE	NEUTRAL	NEGATIVE

REFLECT ON WHAT HAS CHANGED IN YOUR LIFE SINCE THIS TIME LAST YEAR. WHAT ARE YOU HAPPY ABOUT? WHAT DO YOU WISH YOU COULD CHANGE?

THIS WEEK'S HAPPY MOMENT

THIS WEEK I'M GRATEFUL FOR

WEEKLY GOALS

1 -------------------------------------

----

2 -------------------------------------

----

3 -------------------------------------

TO DO

- • -------------------------------------
- • -------------------------------------
- • -------------------------------------
- • -------------------------------------
- • -------------------------------------
- • -------------------------------------
- • -------------------------------------
- • -------------------------------------
- • -------------------------------------
- • -------------------------------------

You must be the best judge of your own happiness.

—JANE AUSTEN, *EMMA*

TRACK YOUR
MOOD

SUNDAY AM PM
MONDAY AM PM
TUESDAY AM PM
WEDNESDAY AM PM
THURSDAY AM PM
FRIDAY AM PM
SATURDAY AM PM

MARCH 2023

Mo	Tu	We	Th	Fr	Sa	Su
		1	2	3	4	5
6	7	8	9	10	11	12
13	14	15	16	17	18	19
20	21	22	23	24	25	26
27	28	29	30	31		

MAY 2023

Mo	Tu	We	Th	Fr	Sa	Su
1	2	3	4	5	6	7
8	9	10	11	12	13	14
15	16	17	18	19	20	21
22	23	24	25	26	27	28
29	30	31				

(COLOR) SCALE

NOTES

APRIL

10 | **MONDAY**   *Easter Monday (AUS, CAN, NZ, UK except SCT)*

11 | **TUESDAY**

12 | **WEDNESDAY**

13 | **THURSDAY**

14 | **FRIDAY**

15 | **SATURDAY**

16 | **SUNDAY**

REFLECT ON YOUR MOODS THIS WEEK.

WHAT IMPACTED YOUR MOOD?

POSITIVE	NEUTRAL	NEGATIVE

WHAT IS ONE THING IN YOUR ROUTINE THAT YOU CAN CHANGE (EVEN JUST FOR THIS WEEK) TO GIVE YOURSELF MORE TIME TO RELAX AND RECHARGE?

THIS WEEK'S HAPPY MOMENT

THIS WEEK I'M GRATEFUL FOR

WEEKLY GOALS

1 ....
....

2 ....
....

3 ....
....

TO DO

- ....
- ....
- ....
- ....
- ....
- ....
- ....
- ....
- ....
- ....

> Realize that this very body...with its aches and its pleasures...is exactly what we need to be fully human, fully awake, fully alive.
>
> —PEMA CHÖDRÖN

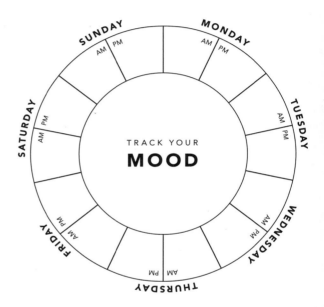

TRACK YOUR **MOOD**

MARCH 2023

Mo	Tu	We	Th	Fr	Sa	Su
		1	2	3	4	5
6	7	8	9	10	11	12
13	14	15	16	17	18	19
20	21	22	23	24	25	26
27	28	29	30	31		

MAY 2023

Mo	Tu	We	Th	Fr	Sa	Su
1	2	3	4	5	6	7
8	9	10	11	12	13	14
15	16	17	18	19	20	21
22	23	24	25	26	27	28
29	30	31				

(COLOR) SCALE

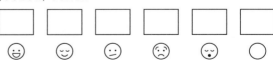

NOTES

17 MONDAY

18 TUESDAY *Tax Day*

19 WEDNESDAY

20 THURSDAY

21 FRIDAY *Eid al-Fitr begins*

22 SATURDAY *Earth Day*

23 SUNDAY

REFLECT ON YOUR MOODS THIS WEEK.

WHAT IMPACTED YOUR MOOD?

POSITIVE	NEUTRAL	NEGATIVE

WRITE OUT A LIST OF SOME OF YOUR FAVORITE MEMORIES. IN
DIFFICULT TIMES IT IS VALUABLE TO REMIND YOURSELF OF WONDERFUL
EXPERIENCES. WHY ARE THEY SPECIAL TO YOU?

THIS WEEK'S HAPPY MOMENT

THIS WEEK I'M GRATEFUL FOR

WEEKLY GOALS

1 ---------------------------------
  ----
2 ---------------------------------
  ----
3 ---------------------------------

TO DO

- ---------------------------------
- ---------------------------------
- ---------------------------------
- ---------------------------------
- ---------------------------------
- ---------------------------------
- ---------------------------------
- ---------------------------------
- ---------------------------------
- ---------------------------------

Happiness is not a station you arrive at, but a manner of traveling.

—MARGARET LEE RUNBECK

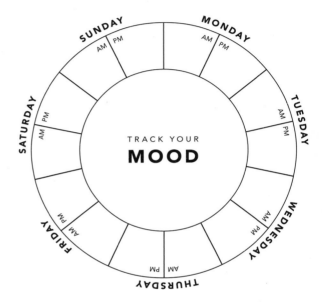

TRACK YOUR
MOOD

MARCH 2023

Mo	Tu	We	Th	Fr	Sa	Su
		1	2	3	4	5
6	7	8	9	10	11	12
13	14	15	16	17	18	19
20	21	22	23	24	25	26
27	28	29	30	31		

MAY 2023

Mo	Tu	We	Th	Fr	Sa	Su
1	2	3	4	5	6	7
8	9	10	11	12	13	14
15	16	17	18	19	20	21
22	23	24	25	26	27	28
29	30	31				

(COLOR) SCALE

NOTES

APRIL

24 MONDAY

25 TUESDAY *Anzac Day (AUS, NZ)*

26 WEDNESDAY

27 THURSDAY

28 FRIDAY *Workers' Memorial Day (UK)*

29 SATURDAY

30 SUNDAY

REFLECT ON YOUR MOODS THIS WEEK.

WHAT IMPACTED YOUR MOOD?

POSITIVE	NEUTRAL	NEGATIVE

MONTHLY REFLECTION: WHAT MOST AFFECTED YOUR MOOD THIS MONTH?

THIS WEEK'S HAPPY MOMENT

THIS WEEK I'M GRATEFUL FOR

MAY

MONDAY	TUESDAY	WEDNESDAY	THURSDAY	FRIDAY
1	2	3	4	5 *Cinco de Mayo*
8	9	10	11	12
15	16	17	18	19
22 *Victoria Day (CAN)*	23	24	25 *Shavuot begins*	26
29 *Memorial Day (USA); Spring Bank Holiday (UK)*	30	31		

19

20

21

22

23

SATURDAY	SUNDAY
6	7
13	14
	Mother's Day (USA, AUS, CAN, NZ)
20	21
Armed Forces Day	
27	28

19
20
21
22
23

NOTES

MONTHLY GOAL TRACKER

GOAL:

(1) (2) (3) (4) (5) (6) (7) (8) (9) (10) (11) (12) (13) (14)
(15) (16) (17) (18) (19) (20) (21) (22) (23) (24) (25) (26) (27) (28)
(29) (30) (31)

GOAL:

(1) (2) (3) (4) (5) (6) (7) (8) (9) (10) (11) (12) (13) (14)
(15) (16) (17) (18) (19) (20) (21) (22) (23) (24) (25) (26) (27) (28)
(29) (30) (31)

GOAL:

(1) (2) (3) (4) (5) (6) (7) (8) (9) (10) (11) (12) (13) (14)
(15) (16) (17) (18) (19) (20) (21) (22) (23) (24) (25) (26) (27) (28)
(29) (30) (31)

WEEKLY GOALS

1
- -

- -
2
- -

- -
3
- -

- -

TO DO

- • -
- • -
- • -
- • -
- • -
- • -
- • -
- • -
- • -
- • -

The only Zen you can find on the tops of mountains is the Zen you bring up there.

—ROBERT M. PIRSIG

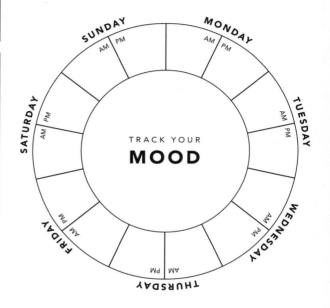

TRACK YOUR
MOOD

APRIL 2023

Mo	Tu	We	Th	Fr	Sa	Su
					1	2
3	4	5	6	7	8	9
10	11	12	13	14	15	16
17	18	19	20	21	22	23
24	25	26	27	28	29	30

JUNE 2023

Mo	Tu	We	Th	Fr	Sa	Su
			1	2	3	4
5	6	7	8	9	10	11
12	13	14	15	16	17	18
19	20	21	22	23	24	25
26	27	28	29	30		

(COLOR) SCALE

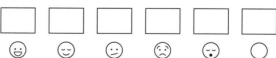

NOTES

MAY

1 | MONDAY

2 | TUESDAY

3 | WEDNESDAY

4 | THURSDAY

5 | FRIDAY   *Cinco de Mayo*

6 | SATURDAY

7 | SUNDAY

REFLECT ON YOUR MOODS THIS WEEK.

WHAT IMPACTED YOUR MOOD?

POSITIVE	NEUTRAL	NEGATIVE

LIST SOME OF THE NEGATIVE EMOTIONS YOU'VE HAD THIS WEEK. IT IS
IMPORTANT TO ACKNOWLEDGE THE VALIDITY OF ALL YOUR EMOTIONS,
EVEN THE DIFFICULT ONES. FEELINGS—PLEASANT OR PAINFUL—ARE WHAT
MAKE YOU HUMAN.

THIS WEEK'S HAPPY MOMENT

THIS WEEK I'M GRATEFUL FOR

WEEKLY GOALS

1

2

3

> Step out of the history that is holding you back.
> Step into the new story you are willing to create.
>
> —OPRAH WINFREY

TO DO

-
-
-
-
-
-
-
-
-

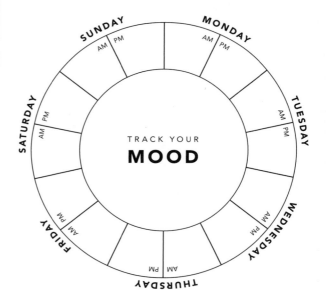

TRACK YOUR
MOOD

SUNDAY · MONDAY · TUESDAY · WEDNESDAY · THURSDAY · FRIDAY · SATURDAY (AM/PM)

APRIL 2023

Mo	Tu	We	Th	Fr	Sa	Su
					1	2
3	4	5	6	7	8	9
10	11	12	13	14	15	16
17	18	19	20	21	22	23
24	25	26	27	28	29	30

JUNE 2023

Mo	Tu	We	Th	Fr	Sa	Su
			1	2	3	4
5	6	7	8	9	10	11
12	13	14	15	16	17	18
19	20	21	22	23	24	25
26	27	28	29	30		

(COLOR) SCALE

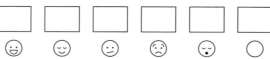

NOTES

MAY

8 | **MONDAY**

9 | **TUESDAY**

10 | **WEDNESDAY**

11 | **THURSDAY**

12 | **FRIDAY**

13 | **SATURDAY**

14 | **SUNDAY** *Mother's Day (USA, AUS, CAN, NZ)*

REFLECT ON YOUR MOODS THIS WEEK.

WHAT IMPACTED YOUR MOOD?

POSITIVE	NEUTRAL	NEGATIVE

WHAT ARE THREE WAYS YOU CAN IMPROVE YOUR MOOD THIS COMING WEEK?

THIS WEEK'S HAPPY MOMENT

THIS WEEK I'M GRATEFUL FOR

WEEKLY GOALS

1

2

3

TO DO

• -----------------------------------
• -----------------------------------
• -----------------------------------
• -----------------------------------
• -----------------------------------
• -----------------------------------
• -----------------------------------
• -----------------------------------
• -----------------------------------
• -----------------------------------

When we strive to become better than we are, everything around us becomes better too.

—PAULO COELHO

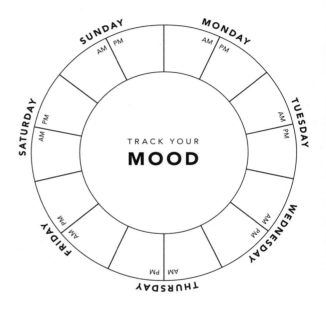

TRACK YOUR
MOOD

APRIL 2023

Mo	Tu	We	Th	Fr	Sa	Su
					1	2
3	4	5	6	7	8	9
10	11	12	13	14	15	16
17	18	19	20	21	22	23
24	25	26	27	28	29	30

JUNE 2023

Mo	Tu	We	Th	Fr	Sa	Su
			1	2	3	4
5	6	7	8	9	10	11
12	13	14	15	16	17	18
19	20	21	22	23	24	25
26	27	28	29	30		

(COLOR) SCALE

NOTES

15 MONDAY

16 TUESDAY

17 WEDNESDAY

18 THURSDAY

19 FRIDAY

20 SATURDAY *Armed Forces Day*

21 SUNDAY

REFLECT ON YOUR MOODS THIS WEEK.

WHAT IMPACTED YOUR MOOD?

POSITIVE	NEUTRAL	NEGATIVE

MAKE A PLAN TO REACH OUT TO SOMEONE YOU LOVE THIS WEEK.
STRENGTHENING YOUR CONNECTIONS CAN HELP YOU FEEL MORE
GROUNDED.

THIS WEEK'S HAPPY MOMENT

THIS WEEK I'M GRATEFUL FOR

WEEKLY GOALS

1 ....
....
2 ....
....
3 ....
....

TO DO

- • ....
- • ....
- • ....
- • ....
- • ....
- • ....
- • ....
- • ....
- • ....
- • ....

The thing that is really hard, and really amazing, is giving up on being perfect and beginning the work of becoming yourself.

—ANNA QUINDLEN

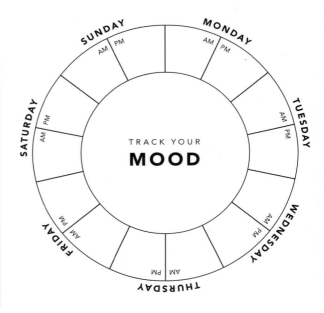

APRIL 2023

Mo	Tu	We	Th	Fr	Sa	Su
					1	2
3	4	5	6	7	8	9
10	11	12	13	14	15	16
17	18	19	20	21	22	23
24	25	26	27	28	29	30

JUNE 2023

Mo	Tu	We	Th	Fr	Sa	Su
			1	2	3	4
5	6	7	8	9	10	11
12	13	14	15	16	17	18
19	20	21	22	23	24	25
26	27	28	29	30		

(COLOR) SCALE

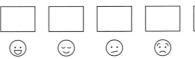

NOTES

MAY

22 MONDAY *Victoria Day (CAN)*

23 TUESDAY

24 WEDNESDAY

25 THURSDAY *Shavuot begins*

26 FRIDAY

27 SATURDAY

28 SUNDAY

REFLECT ON YOUR MOODS THIS WEEK.

WHAT IMPACTED YOUR MOOD?

POSITIVE	NEUTRAL	NEGATIVE

MONTHLY REFLECTION: WHAT MOST AFFECTED YOUR MOOD THIS MONTH?

THIS WEEK'S HAPPY MOMENT

THIS WEEK I'M GRATEFUL FOR

JUNE

MONDAY	TUESDAY	WEDNESDAY	THURSDAY	FRIDAY
			1	2
5	6	7	8	9
12	13	14 *Flag Day*	15	16
19 *Juneteenth*	20	21 *Summer begins (Northern Hemisphere)*	22	23
26	27	28 *Eid al-Adha begins*	29	30

23
24
25
26
27

SATURDAY	SUNDAY
3	4
10	11
17	18 *Father's Day (USA, CAN, UK)*
24	25

23
24
25
26

NOTES

MONTHLY GOAL TRACKER

GOAL:

1 2 3 4 5 6 7 8 9 10 11 12 13 14
15 16 17 18 19 20 21 22 23 24 25 26 27 28
29 30 31

GOAL:

1 2 3 4 5 6 7 8 9 10 11 12 13 14
15 16 17 18 19 20 21 22 23 24 25 26 27 28
29 30 31

GOAL:

1 2 3 4 5 6 7 8 9 10 11 12 13 14
15 16 17 18 19 20 21 22 23 24 25 26 27 28
29 30 31

WEEKLY GOALS

1 ....
....

2 ....
....

3 ....
....

TO DO

- ....
- ....
- ....
- ....
- ....
- ....
- ....
- ....
- ....
- ....

What soap is for the body, tears are for the soul.

—JEWISH PROVERB

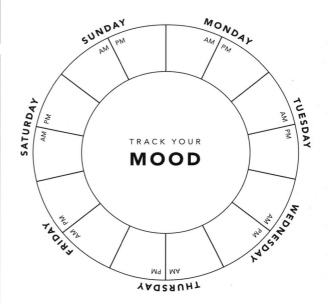

TRACK YOUR
MOOD

MAY 2023

Mo	Tu	We	Th	Fr	Sa	Su
1	2	3	4	5	6	7
8	9	10	11	12	13	14
15	16	17	18	19	20	21
22	23	24	25	26	27	28
29	30	31				

JULY 2023

Mo	Tu	We	Th	Fr	Sa	Su
					1	2
3	4	5	6	7	8	9
10	11	12	13	14	15	16
17	18	19	20	21	22	23
24	25	26	27	28	29	30
31						

(COLOR) SCALE

NOTES

MAY/JUNE

29 **MONDAY**   *Memorial Day (USA)*
Spring Bank Holiday (UK)

30 **TUESDAY**

31 **WEDNESDAY**

1 **THURSDAY**

2 **FRIDAY**

3 **SATURDAY**

4 **SUNDAY**

REFLECT ON YOUR MOODS THIS WEEK.

WHAT IMPACTED YOUR MOOD?

POSITIVE	NEUTRAL	NEGATIVE

CHECK IN WITH YOURSELF ABOUT THE BIG STRESSORS IN YOUR LIFE THIS WEEK. HOW CAN YOU PREPARE NOW TO SAVE YOURSELF SOME WORRY LATER?

THIS WEEK'S HAPPY MOMENT

THIS WEEK I'M GRATEFUL FOR

WEEKLY GOALS

1
- -

2
- -

3
- -

- -

TO DO

- • -
- • -
- • -
- • -
- • -
- • -
- • -
- • -
- • -
- • -

Rise & shine! Or rise & sulk! Or rise & weep! Or rise & roar! But RISE.

—LIN-MANUEL MIRANDA

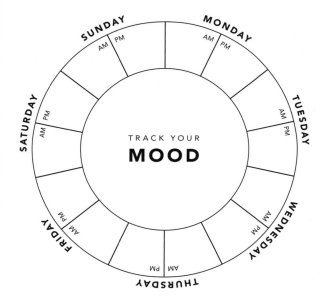

TRACK YOUR
MOOD

MAY 2023

Mo	Tu	We	Th	Fr	Sa	Su
1	2	3	4	5	6	7
8	9	10	11	12	13	14
15	16	17	18	19	20	21
22	23	24	25	26	27	28
29	30	31				

JULY 2023

Mo	Tu	We	Th	Fr	Sa	Su
					1	2
3	4	5	6	7	8	9
10	11	12	13	14	15	16
17	18	19	20	21	22	23
24	25	26	27	28	29	30
31						

(C O L O R)   S C A L E

NOTES

JUNE

5 | MONDAY

6 | TUESDAY

7 | WEDNESDAY

8 | THURSDAY

9 | FRIDAY

10 | SATURDAY

11 | SUNDAY

REFLECT ON YOUR MOODS THIS WEEK.

WHAT IMPACTED YOUR MOOD?

POSITIVE	NEUTRAL	NEGATIVE

MAKE A LIST OF SKILLS YOU HAVE THAT YOU THINK ARE THE MOST
IMPRESSIVE. APPRECIATE THE WORK YOU'VE DONE TO CREATE THOSE
SKILLS!

THIS WEEK'S HAPPY MOMENT

THIS WEEK I'M GRATEFUL FOR

WEEKLY GOALS

1

2

3

TO DO

- -------------------------------------
- -------------------------------------
- -------------------------------------
- -------------------------------------
- -------------------------------------
- -------------------------------------
- -------------------------------------
- -------------------------------------
- -------------------------------------
- -------------------------------------

You must find the place inside yourself where nothing is impossible.

—DEEPAK CHOPRA

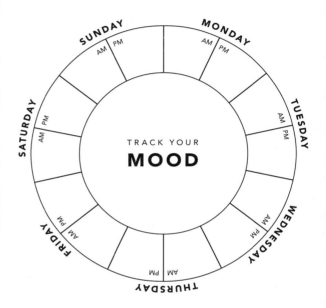

TRACK YOUR
MOOD

MAY 2023

Mo	Tu	We	Th	Fr	Sa	Su
1	2	3	4	5	6	7
8	9	10	11	12	13	14
15	16	17	18	19	20	21
22	23	24	25	26	27	28
29	30	31				

JULY 2023

Mo	Tu	We	Th	Fr	Sa	Su
					1	2
3	4	5	6	7	8	9
10	11	12	13	14	15	16
17	18	19	20	21	22	23
24	25	26	27	28	29	30
31						

(COLOR) SCALE

NOTES

JUNE

12 **MONDAY**

13 **TUESDAY**

14 **WEDNESDAY** *Flag Day*

15 **THURSDAY**

16 **FRIDAY**

17 **SATURDAY**

18 **SUNDAY** *Father's Day (USA, CAN, UK)*

REFLECT ON YOUR MOODS THIS WEEK.

WHAT IMPACTED YOUR MOOD?

POSITIVE	NEUTRAL	NEGATIVE

SUMMER MEANS WARM WEATHER AND LONGER DAYS—BUT THAT DOESN'T
MEAN ALL STRESS DISAPPEARS. WHAT CAN YOU DO THIS WEEK TO MAKE
SURE YOU HAVE THE TIME AND ENERGY TO ENJOY THE START OF THE
SEASON?

THIS WEEK'S HAPPY MOMENT

THIS WEEK I'M GRATEFUL FOR

WEEKLY GOALS

1 ....
....

2 ....
....

3 ....
....

TO DO

• ....
• ....
• ....
• ....
• ....
• ....
• ....
• ....
• ....
• ....

I know of a cure for everything: salt water... Sweat, tears, or the salt sea.

—ISAK DINESEN, "THE DELUGE AT NORDERNEY"

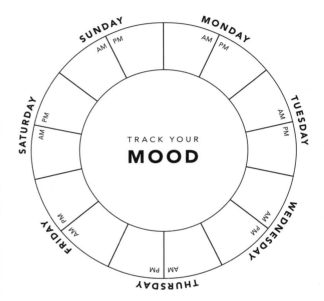

TRACK YOUR
MOOD

MAY 2023

Mo	Tu	We	Th	Fr	Sa	Su
1	2	3	4	5	6	7
8	9	10	11	12	13	14
15	16	17	18	19	20	21
22	23	24	25	26	27	28
29	30	31				

JULY 2023

Mo	Tu	We	Th	Fr	Sa	Su
					1	2
3	4	5	6	7	8	9
10	11	12	13	14	15	16
17	18	19	20	21	22	23
24	25	26	27	28	29	30
31						

(COLOR) SCALE

NOTES

JUNE

19 **MONDAY** *Juneteenth*

20 **TUESDAY**

21 **WEDNESDAY** *Summer begins (Northern Hemisphere)*

22 **THURSDAY**

23 **FRIDAY**

24 **SATURDAY**

25 **SUNDAY**

REFLECT ON YOUR MOODS THIS WEEK.

WHAT IMPACTED YOUR MOOD?

POSITIVE	NEUTRAL	NEGATIVE

WHAT EVENTS OR ACTIVITIES ARE YOU EASILY PRESENT AND ENGAGED IN? WHAT ONES ARE YOU EASILY DISTRACTED IN?

THIS WEEK'S HAPPY MOMENT

THIS WEEK I'M GRATEFUL FOR

WEEKLY GOALS

1 _____

_____

2 _____

_____

3 _____

_____

TO DO

- _____
- _____
- _____
- _____
- _____
- _____
- _____
- _____
- _____
- _____

I am the sole author of the dictionary that defines me.

—ZADIE SMITH

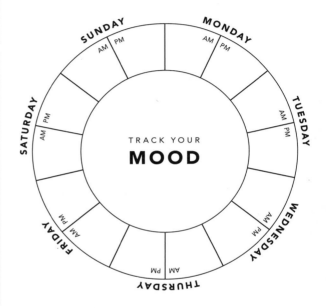

TRACK YOUR
MOOD

MAY 2023

Mo	Tu	We	Th	Fr	Sa	Su
1	2	3	4	5	6	7
8	9	10	11	12	13	14
15	16	17	18	19	20	21
22	23	24	25	26	27	28
29	30	31				

JULY 2023

Mo	Tu	We	Th	Fr	Sa	Su
					1	2
3	4	5	6	7	8	9
10	11	12	13	14	15	16
17	18	19	20	21	22	23
24	25	26	27	28	29	30
31						

(COLOR) SCALE

NOTES

JUNE/JULY

26 | **MONDAY**

27 | **TUESDAY**

28 | **WEDNESDAY** *Eid al-Adha begins*

29 | **THURSDAY**

30 | **FRIDAY**

1 | **SATURDAY** *Canada Day (CAN)*

2 | **SUNDAY**

REFLECT ON YOUR MOODS THIS WEEK.

WHAT IMPACTED YOUR MOOD?

POSITIVE	NEUTRAL	NEGATIVE

MONTHLY REFLECTION: WHAT MOST AFFECTED YOUR MOOD THIS MONTH?

THIS WEEK'S HAPPY MOMENT

THIS WEEK I'M GRATEFUL FOR

JULY

MONDAY	TUESDAY	WEDNESDAY	THURSDAY	FRIDAY
27				
3	4	5	6	7
	Independence Day			
28				
10	11	12	13	14
		Orangemen's Day—Battle of the Boyne (NIR)		
29				
17	18	19	20	21
30				
24	25	26	27	28
31				
31/32				

SATURDAY	SUNDAY
1	2
Canada Day (CAN)	
8	9
15	16
22	23
29	30

27
28
29
30
31

NOTES

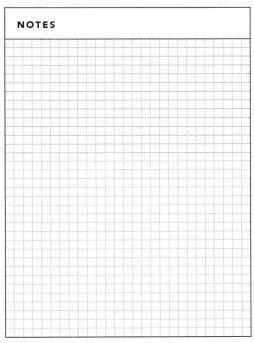

MONTHLY GOAL TRACKER

GOAL:

1 2 3 4 5 6 7 8 9 10 11 12 13 14
15 16 17 18 19 20 21 22 23 24 25 26 27 28
29 30 31

GOAL:

1 2 3 4 5 6 7 8 9 10 11 12 13 14
15 16 17 18 19 20 21 22 23 24 25 26 27 28
29 30 31

GOAL:

1 2 3 4 5 6 7 8 9 10 11 12 13 14
15 16 17 18 19 20 21 22 23 24 25 26 27 28
29 30 31

WEEKLY GOALS

1
- -
- -
2
- -
- -
3
- -
- -

Trust in your deepest strength of all: to be present, to be wakeful.

—JON KABAT-ZINN

TO DO

- • -
- • -
- • -
- • -
- • -
- • -
- • -
- • -
- • -
- • -

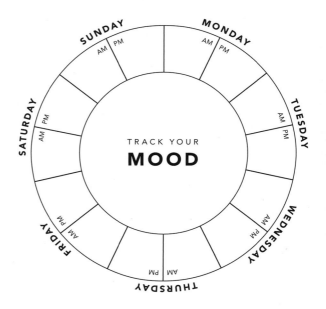

TRACK YOUR
MOOD

JUNE 2023

Mo	Tu	We	Th	Fr	Sa	Su
			1	2	3	4
5	6	7	8	9	10	11
12	13	14	15	16	17	18
19	20	21	22	23	24	25
26	27	28	29	30		

(COLOR) SCALE

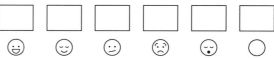

AUGUST 2023

Mo	Tu	We	Th	Fr	Sa	Su
	1	2	3	4	5	6
7	8	9	10	11	12	13
14	15	16	17	18	19	20
21	22	23	24	25	26	27
28	29	30	31			

NOTES

JULY

3 | **MONDAY**

4 | **TUESDAY**   *Independence Day*

5 | **WEDNESDAY**

6 | **THURSDAY**

7 | **FRIDAY**

8 | **SATURDAY**

9 | **SUNDAY**

REFLECT ON YOUR MOODS THIS WEEK.

WHAT IMPACTED YOUR MOOD?

POSITIVE	NEUTRAL	NEGATIVE

MID-YEAR REFLECTION: LIST SOME WAYS YOU'VE GROWN SINCE THE BEGINNING OF THE YEAR.

THIS WEEK'S HAPPY MOMENT

THIS WEEK I'M GRATEFUL FOR

WEEKLY GOALS

1

2

3

TO DO

- -----------------------------------
- -----------------------------------
- -----------------------------------
- -----------------------------------
- -----------------------------------
- -----------------------------------
- -----------------------------------
- -----------------------------------
- -----------------------------------
- -----------------------------------

Life is 10 percent what happens to me and 90 percent how I react to it.

—CHARLES R. SWINDOLL

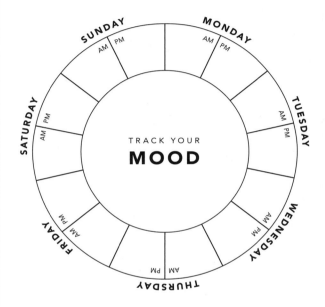

JUNE 2023

Mo	Tu	We	Th	Fr	Sa	Su
			1	2	3	4
5	6	7	8	9	10	11
12	13	14	15	16	17	18
19	20	21	22	23	24	25
26	27	28	29	30		

(COLOR) SCALE

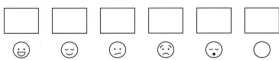

AUGUST 2023

Mo	Tu	We	Th	Fr	Sa	Su
	1	2	3	4	5	6
7	8	9	10	11	12	13
14	15	16	17	18	19	20
21	22	23	24	25	26	27
28	29	30	31			

NOTES

JULY

10 | **MONDAY**

11 | **TUESDAY**

12 | **WEDNESDAY**   *Orangemen's Day—Battle of the Boyne (NIR)*

13 | **THURSDAY**

14 | **FRIDAY**

15 | **SATURDAY**

16 | **SUNDAY**

REFLECT ON YOUR MOODS THIS WEEK.

WHAT IMPACTED YOUR MOOD?

POSITIVE	NEUTRAL	NEGATIVE

STRESS CAN OFTEN BE CAUSED BY YOUR ENVIRONMENT. JOT DOWN
SOME WAYS TO MAKE YOUR WORKSPACE OR HOME MORE WELCOMING
THIS WEEK.

THIS WEEK'S HAPPY MOMENT

THIS WEEK I'M GRATEFUL FOR

WEEKLY GOALS

1 ....

....

2 ....

....

3 ....

....

TO DO

- ....
- ....
- ....
- ....
- ....
- ....
- ....
- ....
- ....
- ....

> Whatever you do in life, remember: Think higher and feel deeper. It cannot be bad if you do that.
>
> —ELIE WIESEL

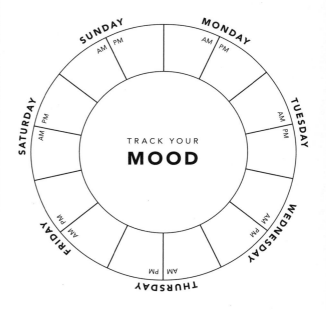

TRACK YOUR
MOOD

JUNE 2023

Mo	Tu	We	Th	Fr	Sa	Su
			1	2	3	4
5	6	7	8	9	10	11
12	13	14	15	16	17	18
19	20	21	22	23	24	25
26	27	28	29	30		

AUGUST 2023

Mo	Tu	We	Th	Fr	Sa	Su
	1	2	3	4	5	6
7	8	9	10	11	12	13
14	15	16	17	18	19	20
21	22	23	24	25	26	27
28	29	30	31			

(COLOR) SCALE

NOTES

JULY

17 MONDAY

18 TUESDAY

19 WEDNESDAY

20 THURSDAY

21 FRIDAY

22 SATURDAY

23 SUNDAY

REFLECT ON YOUR MOODS THIS WEEK.

WHAT IMPACTED YOUR MOOD?

POSITIVE	NEUTRAL	NEGATIVE

JULY 17—JULY 23   WEEK 30 / 2023

THINK ABOUT THE MOMENTS YOU FEEL MOST CONFIDENT. WHAT ARE YOU
DOING? WHY ARE THOSE MOMENTS SO SPECIAL?

THIS WEEK'S HAPPY MOMENT

THIS WEEK I'M GRATEFUL FOR

WEEKLY GOALS

1

2

3

TO DO

- ----------------------------------
- ----------------------------------
- ----------------------------------
- ----------------------------------
- ----------------------------------
- ----------------------------------
- ----------------------------------
- ----------------------------------
- ----------------------------------
- ----------------------------------

Happiness often sneaks in through a door you didn't know you left open.

—JOHN BARRYMORE

TRACK YOUR
MOOD

SUNDAY AM PM
MONDAY AM PM
TUESDAY AM PM
WEDNESDAY AM PM
THURSDAY AM PM
FRIDAY AM PM
SATURDAY AM PM

JUNE 2023

Mo	Tu	We	Th	Fr	Sa	Su
			1	2	3	4
5	6	7	8	9	10	11
12	13	14	15	16	17	18
19	20	21	22	23	24	25
26	27	28	29	30		

AUGUST 2023

Mo	Tu	We	Th	Fr	Sa	Su
	1	2	3	4	5	6
7	8	9	10	11	12	13
14	15	16	17	18	19	20
21	22	23	24	25	26	27
28	29	30	31			

(COLOR) SCALE

NOTES

JULY

24 | MONDAY

25 | TUESDAY

26 | WEDNESDAY

27 | THURSDAY

28 | FRIDAY

29 | SATURDAY

30 | SUNDAY

REFLECT ON YOUR MOODS THIS WEEK.

WHAT IMPACTED YOUR MOOD?

POSITIVE

NEUTRAL

NEGATIVE

MONTHLY REFLECTION: WHAT MOST AFFECTED YOUR MOOD THIS MONTH?

THIS WEEK'S HAPPY MOMENT

THIS WEEK I'M GRATEFUL FOR

AUGUST

MONDAY	TUESDAY	WEDNESDAY	THURSDAY	FRIDAY
	1	2	3	4
7 *Summer Bank Holiday (SCT)*	8	9	10	11
14	15	16	17	18
21	22	23	24	25
28 *Summer Bank Holiday (UK except SCT)*	29	30	31	

32
33
34
35
36

SATURDAY	SUNDAY
5	6
12	13
19	20
26	27

32
33
34
35

NOTES

MONTHLY GOAL TRACKER

GOAL: --

(1) (2) (3) (4) (5) (6) (7) (8) (9) (10) (11) (12) (13) (14)
(15) (16) (17) (18) (19) (20) (21) (22) (23) (24) (25) (26) (27) (28)
(29) (30) (31)

GOAL: --

(1) (2) (3) (4) (5) (6) (7) (8) (9) (10) (11) (12) (13) (14)
(15) (16) (17) (18) (19) (20) (21) (22) (23) (24) (25) (26) (27) (28)
(29) (30) (31)

GOAL: --

(1) (2) (3) (4) (5) (6) (7) (8) (9) (10) (11) (12) (13) (14)
(15) (16) (17) (18) (19) (20) (21) (22) (23) (24) (25) (26) (27) (28)
(29) (30) (31)

WEEKLY GOALS

1 -----------------------------------

----

2 -----------------------------------

----

3 -----------------------------------

TO DO

- • -----------------------------------
- • -----------------------------------
- • -----------------------------------
- • -----------------------------------
- • -----------------------------------
- • -----------------------------------
- • -----------------------------------
- • -----------------------------------
- • -----------------------------------
- • -----------------------------------

Expect trouble as an inevitable part of life and when it comes, hold your head high, look it squarely in the eye, and say, "I will be bigger than you. You cannot defeat me."

—ANN LANDERS

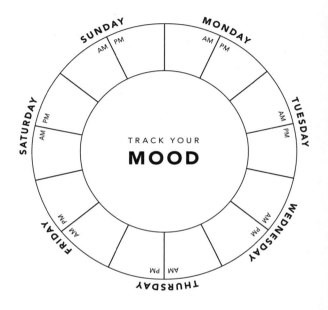

TRACK YOUR **MOOD**

JULY 2023

Mo	Tu	We	Th	Fr	Sa	Su
					1	2
3	4	5	6	7	8	9
10	11	12	13	14	15	16
17	18	19	20	21	22	23
24	25	26	27	28	29	30
31						

SEPTEMBER 2023

Mo	Tu	We	Th	Fr	Sa	Su
				1	2	3
4	5	6	7	8	9	10
11	12	13	14	15	16	17
18	19	20	21	22	23	24
25	26	27	28	29	30	

(COLOR) SCALE

NOTES

JULY/AUGUST

WEEK 32 / **2023**

31 | MONDAY

1 | TUESDAY

2 | WEDNESDAY

3 | THURSDAY

4 | FRIDAY

5 | SATURDAY

6 | SUNDAY

REFLECT ON YOUR MOODS THIS WEEK.

WHAT IMPACTED YOUR MOOD?

POSITIVE	NEUTRAL	NEGATIVE

WRITE DOWN A HANDFUL OF IDEAS FOR PHYSICAL ACTIVITIES YOU
COULD DO THIS WEEK. RECONNECTING WITH YOUR BODY IS A GREAT WAY
TO GET OUT OF A STRESSED HEADSPACE.

THIS WEEK'S HAPPY MOMENT

THIS WEEK I'M GRATEFUL FOR

WEEKLY GOALS

1

2

3

TO DO

- -------------------------------------
- -------------------------------------
- -------------------------------------
- -------------------------------------
- -------------------------------------
- -------------------------------------
- -------------------------------------
- -------------------------------------
- -------------------------------------
- -------------------------------------

Sometimes your joy is the source of your smile, but sometimes your smile can be the source of your joy.

—THICH NHAT HANH

TRACK YOUR MOOD

SUNDAY AM PM
MONDAY AM PM
TUESDAY AM PM
WEDNESDAY AM PM
THURSDAY AM PM
FRIDAY AM PM
SATURDAY AM PM

JULY 2023

Mo	Tu	We	Th	Fr	Sa	Su
					1	2
3	4	5	6	7	8	9
10	11	12	13	14	15	16
17	18	19	20	21	22	23
24	25	26	27	28	29	30
31						

SEPTEMBER 2023

Mo	Tu	We	Th	Fr	Sa	Su
				1	2	3
4	5	6	7	8	9	10
11	12	13	14	15	16	17
18	19	20	21	22	23	24
25	26	27	28	29	30	

(COLOR) SCALE

NOTES

AUGUST

7 | **MONDAY**   *Summer Bank Holiday (SCT)*

8 | **TUESDAY**

9 | **WEDNESDAY**

10 | **THURSDAY**

11 | **FRIDAY**

12 | **SATURDAY**

13 | **SUNDAY**

REFLECT ON YOUR MOODS THIS WEEK.

WHAT IMPACTED YOUR MOOD?

POSITIVE	NEUTRAL	NEGATIVE

WHAT ARE SOME HABITS YOU'VE CHANGED THIS YEAR TO IMPROVE YOUR MOOD? ARE THEY STILL HELPING? ARE THERE ANY YOU SHOULD COME BACK TO WITH A NEW APPROACH?

THIS WEEK'S HAPPY MOMENT

THIS WEEK I'M GRATEFUL FOR

WEEKLY GOALS

1

2

3

TO DO

• --
• --
• --
• --
• --
• --
• --
• --
• --
• --

In three words I can sum up everything I've learned about life: It goes on.

—ROBERT FROST

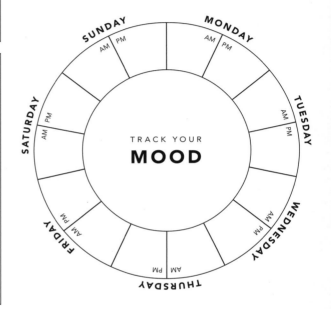

JULY 2023

Mo	Tu	We	Th	Fr	Sa	Su
					1	2
3	4	5	6	7	8	9
10	11	12	13	14	15	16
17	18	19	20	21	22	23
24	25	26	27	28	29	30
31						

SEPTEMBER 2023

Mo	Tu	We	Th	Fr	Sa	Su
				1	2	3
4	5	6	7	8	9	10
11	12	13	14	15	16	17
18	19	20	21	22	23	24
25	26	27	28	29	30	

(COLOR) SCALE

NOTES

AUGUST

14 | **MONDAY**

15 | **TUESDAY**

16 | **WEDNESDAY**

17 | **THURSDAY**

18 | **FRIDAY**

19 | **SATURDAY**

20 | **SUNDAY**

REFLECT ON YOUR MOODS THIS WEEK.

WHAT IMPACTED YOUR MOOD?

POSITIVE	NEUTRAL	NEGATIVE

WRITE DOWN SOME THINGS (ACTIVITIES, PEOPLE, ETC.) YOU MISS. IF YOU ARE ABLE TO, PUT A PLAN IN PLACE TO START ADDING SOME OF THOSE THINGS BACK INTO YOUR LIFE THIS WEEK.

THIS WEEK'S HAPPY MOMENT

THIS WEEK I'M GRATEFUL FOR

WEEKLY GOALS

1

2

3

TO DO

- --
- --
- --
- --
- --
- --
- --
- --
- --
- --

You have within you, right now, everything you need to deal with whatever the world can throw at you.

—BRIAN TRACY

TRACK YOUR
MOOD

SUNDAY · MONDAY · TUESDAY · WEDNESDAY · THURSDAY · FRIDAY · SATURDAY (AM/PM)

JULY 2023

Mo	Tu	We	Th	Fr	Sa	Su
					1	2
3	4	5	6	7	8	9
10	11	12	13	14	15	16
17	18	19	20	21	22	23
24	25	26	27	28	29	30
31						

SEPTEMBER 2023

Mo	Tu	We	Th	Fr	Sa	Su
				1	2	3
4	5	6	7	8	9	10
11	12	13	14	15	16	17
18	19	20	21	22	23	24
25	26	27	28	29	30	

(COLOR) SCALE

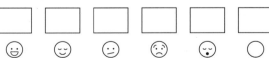

NOTES

AUGUST

21 | MONDAY

22 | TUESDAY

23 | WEDNESDAY

24 | THURSDAY

25 | FRIDAY

26 | SATURDAY

27 | SUNDAY

REFLECT ON YOUR MOODS THIS WEEK.

WHAT IMPACTED YOUR MOOD?

POSITIVE	NEUTRAL	NEGATIVE

FAILURE IS JUST AS IMPORTANT AS SUCCESS AT MAKING YOU A MORE
WELL-ROUNDED PERSON. TAKE A MOMENT TO JOT DOWN SOME OF YOUR
MOST VALUABLE SUCCESSES AND MOST VALUABLE FAILURES.

THIS WEEK'S HAPPY MOMENT

THIS WEEK I'M GRATEFUL FOR

WEEKLY GOALS

1 _____
_____

2 _____
_____

3 _____
_____

TO DO

- _____
- _____
- _____
- _____
- _____
- _____
- _____
- _____
- _____
- _____

Life is not a matter of holding good cards, but of playing a poor hand well.

—JOSH BILLINGS

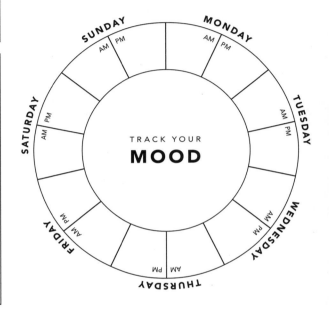

TRACK YOUR
MOOD

JULY 2023

Mo	Tu	We	Th	Fr	Sa	Su
					1	2
3	4	5	6	7	8	9
10	11	12	13	14	15	16
17	18	19	20	21	22	23
24	25	26	27	28	29	30
31						

SEPTEMBER 2023

Mo	Tu	We	Th	Fr	Sa	Su
				1	2	3
4	5	6	7	8	9	10
11	12	13	14	15	16	17
18	19	20	21	22	23	24
25	26	27	28	29	30	

(COLOR) SCALE

NOTES

28 **MONDAY** *Summer Bank Holiday (UK except SCT)*

29 **TUESDAY**

30 **WEDNESDAY**

31 **THURSDAY**

1 **FRIDAY**

2 **SATURDAY**

3 **SUNDAY** *Father's Day (AUS, NZ)*

REFLECT ON YOUR MOODS THIS WEEK.

WHAT IMPACTED YOUR MOOD?

POSITIVE	NEUTRAL	NEGATIVE

MONTHLY REFLECTION: WHAT MOST AFFECTED YOUR MOOD THIS MONTH?

THIS WEEK'S HAPPY MOMENT

THIS WEEK I'M GRATEFUL FOR

SEPTEMBER

MONDAY	TUESDAY	WEDNESDAY	THURSDAY	FRIDAY
				1
4	5	6	7	8
Labor Day (USA, CAN)				
11	12	13	14	15
Patriot Day				*Rosh Hashanah begins*
18	19	20	21	22
25	26	27	28	29
				Sukkot begins

36
37
38
39
40

SATURDAY	SUNDAY
36 2	3
	Father's Day (AUS, NZ)
37 9	10
38 16	17
39 23	24
Autumn begins (Northern Hemisphere)	Yom Kippur begins
30	

NOTES

MONTHLY GOAL TRACKER

GOAL:

----

① ② ③ ④ ⑤ ⑥ ⑦ ⑧ ⑨ ⑩ ⑪ ⑫ ⑬ ⑭
⑮ ⑯ ⑰ ⑱ ⑲ ⑳ ㉑ ㉒ ㉓ ㉔ ㉕ ㉖ ㉗ ㉘
㉙ ㉚ ㉛

GOAL:

----

① ② ③ ④ ⑤ ⑥ ⑦ ⑧ ⑨ ⑩ ⑪ ⑫ ⑬ ⑭
⑮ ⑯ ⑰ ⑱ ⑲ ⑳ ㉑ ㉒ ㉓ ㉔ ㉕ ㉖ ㉗ ㉘
㉙ ㉚ ㉛

GOAL:

----

① ② ③ ④ ⑤ ⑥ ⑦ ⑧ ⑨ ⑩ ⑪ ⑫ ⑬ ⑭
⑮ ⑯ ⑰ ⑱ ⑲ ⑳ ㉑ ㉒ ㉓ ㉔ ㉕ ㉖ ㉗ ㉘
㉙ ㉚ ㉛

WEEKLY GOALS

1 ....

2 ....

3 ....
....

TO DO

- ....
- ....
- ....
- ....
- ....
- ....
- ....
- ....
- ....

AUGUST 2023

Mo	Tu	We	Th	Fr	Sa	Su
	1	2	3	4	5	6
7	8	9	10	11	12	13
14	15	16	17	18	19	20
21	22	23	24	25	26	27
28	29	30	31			

OCTOBER 2023

Mo	Tu	We	Th	Fr	Sa	Su
						1
2	3	4	5	6	7	8
9	10	11	12	13	14	15
16	17	18	19	20	21	22
23	24	25	26	27	28	29
30	31					

Shame corrodes the very part of us that believes we are capable of change.

—BRENÉ BROWN

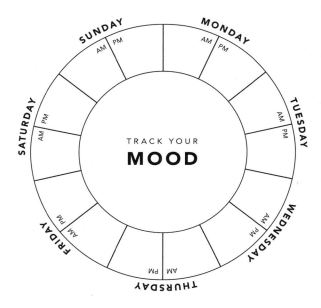

TRACK YOUR
MOOD

(COLOR) SCALE

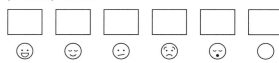

NOTES

SEPTEMBER

4 | **MONDAY**   *Labor Day (USA, CAN)*

5 | **TUESDAY**

6 | **WEDNESDAY**

7 | **THURSDAY**

8 | **FRIDAY**

9 | **SATURDAY**

10 | **SUNDAY**

REFLECT ON YOUR MOODS THIS WEEK.

WHAT IMPACTED YOUR MOOD?

POSITIVE	NEUTRAL	NEGATIVE

SIT DOWN IN A COMFY CHAIR AND CLOSE YOUR EYES. THINK IN SILENCE FOR FIVE MINUTES, LETTING YOUR THOUGHTS COME AND GO BUT NOT LATCHING ON TO ANY OF THEM. WRITE DOWN WHAT THOUGHTS AND IDEAS WERE THE MOST PROMINENT. WHAT DO YOU NOTICE ABOUT WHERE YOUR HEADSPACE IS RIGHT NOW?

THIS WEEK'S HAPPY MOMENT

THIS WEEK I'M GRATEFUL FOR

WEEKLY GOALS

1 ....
   ....

2 ....
   ....

3 ....
   ....

TO DO

- ....
- ....
- ....
- ....
- ....
- ....
- ....
- ....
- ....
- ....
- ....

The challenge is not to be perfect...it's to be whole.

—JANE FONDA

TRACK YOUR
MOOD

SUNDAY · AM PM
MONDAY · AM PM
TUESDAY · AM PM
WEDNESDAY · AM PM
THURSDAY · AM PM
FRIDAY · AM PM
SATURDAY · AM PM

AUGUST 2023

Mo	Tu	We	Th	Fr	Sa	Su
	1	2	3	4	5	6
7	8	9	10	11	12	13
14	15	16	17	18	19	20
21	22	23	24	25	26	27
28	29	30	31			

OCTOBER 2023

Mo	Tu	We	Th	Fr	Sa	Su
						1
2	3	4	5	6	7	8
9	10	11	12	13	14	15
16	17	18	19	20	21	22
23	24	25	26	27	28	29
30	31					

(COLOR) SCALE

NOTES

SEPTEMBER

11 ⋮ **MONDAY** *Patriot Day*

12 ⋮ **TUESDAY**

13 ⋮ **WEDNESDAY**

14 ⋮ **THURSDAY**

15 ⋮ **FRIDAY** *Rosh Hashanah begins*

16 ⋮ **SATURDAY**

17 ⋮ **SUNDAY**

REFLECT ON YOUR MOODS THIS WEEK.

WHAT IMPACTED YOUR MOOD?

POSITIVE	NEUTRAL	NEGATIVE

WHAT ARE THREE WAYS YOU CAN IMPROVE YOUR MOOD THIS COMING WEEK?

THIS WEEK'S HAPPY MOMENT

THIS WEEK I'M GRATEFUL FOR

WEEKLY GOALS

1 _____
_____

2 _____
_____

3 _____
_____

TO DO

- _____
- _____
- _____
- _____
- _____
- _____
- _____
- _____
- _____
- _____

Joy is not in things; it is in us.

—RICHARD WAGNER

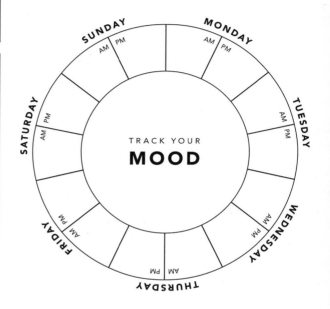

TRACK YOUR
MOOD

SUNDAY · MONDAY · TUESDAY · WEDNESDAY · THURSDAY · FRIDAY · SATURDAY (AM | PM)

AUGUST 2023

Mo	Tu	We	Th	Fr	Sa	Su
	1	2	3	4	5	6
7	8	9	10	11	12	13
14	15	16	17	18	19	20
21	22	23	24	25	26	27
28	29	30	31			

OCTOBER 2023

Mo	Tu	We	Th	Fr	Sa	Su
						1
2	3	4	5	6	7	8
9	10	11	12	13	14	15
16	17	18	19	20	21	22
23	24	25	26	27	28	29
30	31					

(COLOR) SCALE

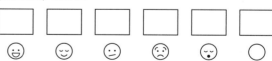

NOTES

SEPTEMBER

18 MONDAY

19 TUESDAY

20 WEDNESDAY

21 THURSDAY

22 FRIDAY

23 SATURDAY *Autumn begins (Northern Hemisphere)*

24 SUNDAY *Yom Kippur begins*

REFLECT ON YOUR MOODS THIS WEEK.

WHAT IMPACTED YOUR MOOD?

POSITIVE	NEUTRAL	NEGATIVE

WHAT IS SOMETHING—A PROJECT, A RELATIONSHIP, A TASK—THAT
YOU THINK IT MAY BE TIME TO STEP AWAY FROM? HOW CAN YOU GIVE
YOURSELF THE SPACE AND FREEDOM TO DO SO IN THE COMING WEEKS?

THIS WEEK'S HAPPY MOMENT

THIS WEEK I'M GRATEFUL FOR

WEEKLY GOALS

1 ....
....
2 ....
....
3 ....
....

TO DO

- ....
- ....
- ....
- ....
- ....
- ....
- ....
- ....
- ....
- ....

If you don't like something, change it. If you can't change it, change your attitude.

—MAYA ANGELOU

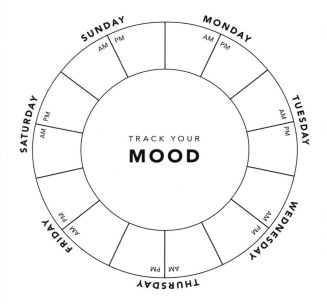

TRACK YOUR
MOOD

AUGUST 2023

Mo	Tu	We	Th	Fr	Sa	Su
	1	2	3	4	5	6
7	8	9	10	11	12	13
14	15	16	17	18	19	20
21	22	23	24	25	26	27
28	29	30	31			

OCTOBER 2023

Mo	Tu	We	Th	Fr	Sa	Su
						1
2	3	4	5	6	7	8
9	10	11	12	13	14	15
16	17	18	19	20	21	22
23	24	25	26	27	28	29
30	31					

(COLOR) SCALE

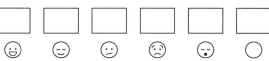

NOTES

25 | MONDAY

26 | TUESDAY

27 | WEDNESDAY

28 | THURSDAY

29 | FRIDAY   *Sukkot begins*

30 | SATURDAY

1 | SUNDAY

REFLECT ON YOUR MOODS THIS WEEK.

WHAT IMPACTED YOUR MOOD?

POSITIVE	NEUTRAL	NEGATIVE

MONTHLY REFLECTION: WHAT MOST AFFECTED YOUR MOOD THIS MONTH?

THIS WEEK'S HAPPY MOMENT

THIS WEEK I'M GRATEFUL FOR

OCTOBER

MONDAY	TUESDAY	WEDNESDAY	THURSDAY	FRIDAY
2	3	4	5	6
9	10	11	12	13
Columbus Day (USA); Indigenous Peoples' Day (USA); Thanksgiving Day (CAN)				
16	17	18	19	20
23	24	25	26	27
30	31			
	Halloween			

41

42

43

44/45

SATURDAY	SUNDAY
	1
7	8
14	15
21	22
28	29

40
41
42
43
44

NOTES

MONTHLY GOAL TRACKER

GOAL:

1 2 3 4 5 6 7 8 9 10 11 12 13 14
15 16 17 18 19 20 21 22 23 24 25 26 27 28
29 30 31

GOAL:

1 2 3 4 5 6 7 8 9 10 11 12 13 14
15 16 17 18 19 20 21 22 23 24 25 26 27 28
29 30 31

GOAL:

1 2 3 4 5 6 7 8 9 10 11 12 13 14
15 16 17 18 19 20 21 22 23 24 25 26 27 28
29 30 31

WEEKLY GOALS

1

2

3

TO DO

- -------------------------------
- -------------------------------
- -------------------------------
- -------------------------------
- -------------------------------
- -------------------------------
- -------------------------------
- -------------------------------
- -------------------------------
- -------------------------------

SEPTEMBER 2023

Mo	Tu	We	Th	Fr	Sa	Su
				1	2	3
4	5	6	7	8	9	10
11	12	13	14	15	16	17
18	19	20	21	22	23	24
25	26	27	28	29	30	

NOVEMBER 2023

Mo	Tu	We	Th	Fr	Sa	Su
		1	2	3	4	5
6	7	8	9	10	11	12
13	14	15	16	17	18	19
20	21	22	23	24	25	26
27	28	29	30			

The way I see it, if you want a rainbow, you gotta put up with the rain.

—DOLLY PARTON

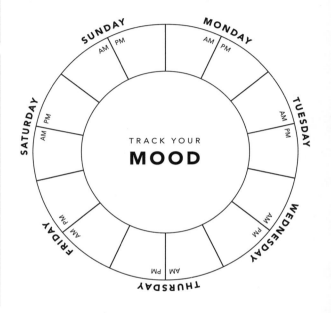

(COLOR) SCALE

NOTES

OCTOBER

2 | MONDAY

3 | TUESDAY

4 | WEDNESDAY

5 | THURSDAY

6 | FRIDAY

7 | SATURDAY

8 | SUNDAY

REFLECT ON YOUR MOODS THIS WEEK.

WHAT IMPACTED YOUR MOOD?

POSITIVE	NEUTRAL	NEGATIVE

FALL IS A TIME OF CHANGE. WHAT CAN YOU ADJUST IN YOUR DAY-TO-DAY LIFE TO POSITIVELY IMPACT YOUR MOOD IN THE UPCOMING MONTHS?

THIS WEEK'S HAPPY MOMENT

THIS WEEK I'M GRATEFUL FOR

WEEKLY GOALS

1 ----------------------------------
----

2 ----------------------------------
----

3 ----------------------------------

TO DO

- • ----------------------------------
- • ----------------------------------
- • ----------------------------------
- • ----------------------------------
- • ----------------------------------
- • ----------------------------------
- • ----------------------------------
- • ----------------------------------
- • ----------------------------------
- • ----------------------------------

Embrace who you are. Literally. Hug yourself.
Accept who you are.

—ELLEN DEGENERES

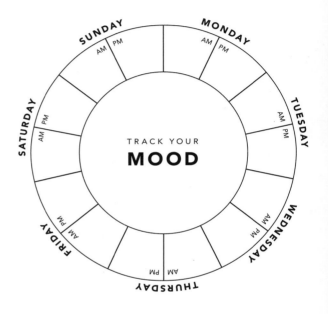

SEPTEMBER 2023

Mo	Tu	We	Th	Fr	Sa	Su
				1	2	3
4	5	6	7	8	9	10
11	12	13	14	15	16	17
18	19	20	21	22	23	24
25	26	27	28	29	30	

NOVEMBER 2023

Mo	Tu	We	Th	Fr	Sa	Su
		1	2	3	4	5
6	7	8	9	10	11	12
13	14	15	16	17	18	19
20	21	22	23	24	25	26
27	28	29	30			

(COLOR) SCALE

NOTES

OCTOBER

9 **MONDAY** *Columbus Day (USA)*
Indigenous Peoples' Day (USA)
Thanksgiving Day (CAN)

10 **TUESDAY**

11 **WEDNESDAY**

12 **THURSDAY**

13 **FRIDAY**

14 **SATURDAY**

15 **SUNDAY**

REFLECT ON YOUR MOODS THIS WEEK.

WHAT IMPACTED YOUR MOOD?

POSITIVE	NEUTRAL	NEGATIVE

BEING BUSY DOESN'T MEAN IGNORING WHAT YOUR BODY AND MIND
NEED. LIST SOME THINGS YOU CAN DO TO TAKE CARE OF YOURSELF THIS
WEEK.

THIS WEEK'S HAPPY MOMENT

THIS WEEK I'M GRATEFUL FOR

WEEKLY GOALS

1
....

....

2
....

....

3
....

....

TO DO

- ....
- ....
- ....
- ....
- ....
- ....
- ....
- ....
- ....
- ....

Anxiety does not empty tomorrow of its sorrows,
but only empties today of its strengths.

—ALEXANDER MCLAREN

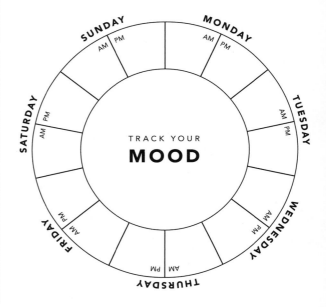

TRACK YOUR
MOOD

SEPTEMBER 2023

Mo	Tu	We	Th	Fr	Sa	Su
				1	2	3
4	5	6	7	8	9	10
11	12	13	14	15	16	17
18	19	20	21	22	23	24
25	26	27	28	29	30	

NOVEMBER 2023

Mo	Tu	We	Th	Fr	Sa	Su
		1	2	3	4	5
6	7	8	9	10	11	12
13	14	15	16	17	18	19
20	21	22	23	24	25	26
27	28	29	30			

(COLOR) SCALE

NOTES

OCTOBER

16 MONDAY

17 TUESDAY

18 WEDNESDAY

19 THURSDAY

20 FRIDAY

21 SATURDAY

22 SUNDAY

REFLECT ON YOUR MOODS THIS WEEK.

WHAT IMPACTED YOUR MOOD?

POSITIVE	NEUTRAL	NEGATIVE

WHICH MOODS DO YOU FIND COUNTERPRODUCTIVE? ARE THERE ANY
PARTICULAR SCENARIOS THAT BRING UP THOSE MOODS FREQUENTLY?

THIS WEEK'S HAPPY MOMENT

THIS WEEK I'M GRATEFUL FOR

WEEKLY GOALS

1
- -
- -
2
- -

- -
3
- -

- -

TO DO

- • -
- • -
- • -
- • -
- • -
- • -
- • -
- • -
- • -
- • -

Our brightest blazes of gladness are commonly kindled by unexpected sparks.

—SAMUEL JOHNSON

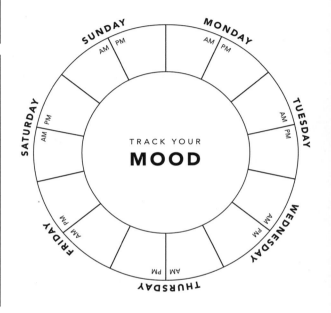

TRACK YOUR
MOOD

SEPTEMBER 2023

Mo	Tu	We	Th	Fr	Sa	Su
				1	2	3
4	5	6	7	8	9	10
11	12	13	14	15	16	17
18	19	20	21	22	23	24
25	26	27	28	29	30	

NOVEMBER 2023

Mo	Tu	We	Th	Fr	Sa	Su
		1	2	3	4	5
6	7	8	9	10	11	12
13	14	15	16	17	18	19
20	21	22	23	24	25	26
27	28	29	30			

(COLOR) SCALE

NOTES

OCTOBER

23 | MONDAY

24 | TUESDAY

25 | WEDNESDAY

26 | THURSDAY

27 | FRIDAY

28 | SATURDAY

29 | SUNDAY

REFLECT ON YOUR MOODS THIS WEEK.

WHAT IMPACTED YOUR MOOD?

POSITIVE	NEUTRAL	NEGATIVE

MONTHLY REFLECTION: WHAT MOST AFFECTED YOUR MOOD THIS MONTH?

THIS WEEK'S HAPPY MOMENT

THIS WEEK I'M GRATEFUL FOR

NOVEMBER

MONDAY	TUESDAY	WEDNESDAY	THURSDAY	FRIDAY
		1	2	3
6	7 *Election Day*	8	9	10
13	14	15	16	17
20	21	22	23 *Thanksgiving Day*	24
27	28	29	30 *St. Andrew's Day (SCT)*	

45
46
47
48
49

SATURDAY	SUNDAY
4	5
	Daylight Saving Time ends (USA, CAN)
11	12
Veterans Day (USA); Remembrance Day (CAN, UK)	*Diwali begins*
18	19
25	26

45
46
47
48

NOTES

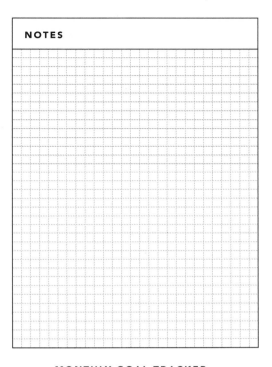

MONTHLY GOAL TRACKER

GOAL: --

(1) (2) (3) (4) (5) (6) (7) (8) (9) (10) (11) (12) (13) (14)
(15) (16) (17) (18) (19) (20) (21) (22) (23) (24) (25) (26) (27) (28)
(29) (30) (31)

GOAL: --

(1) (2) (3) (4) (5) (6) (7) (8) (9) (10) (11) (12) (13) (14)
(15) (16) (17) (18) (19) (20) (21) (22) (23) (24) (25) (26) (27) (28)
(29) (30) (31)

GOAL: --

(1) (2) (3) (4) (5) (6) (7) (8) (9) (10) (11) (12) (13) (14)
(15) (16) (17) (18) (19) (20) (21) (22) (23) (24) (25) (26) (27) (28)
(29) (30) (31)

WEEKLY GOALS

1 ------------------------------
----
2 ------------------------------
----

3 ------------------------------

TO DO

- • ------------------------------
- • ------------------------------
- • ------------------------------
- • ------------------------------
- • ------------------------------
- • ------------------------------
- • ------------------------------
- • ------------------------------
- • ------------------------------
- • ------------------------------

Feel the depths of all the emotions that surface and stick with them, ride them out, until the feelings naturally pass.

—ELLIE NEWMAN

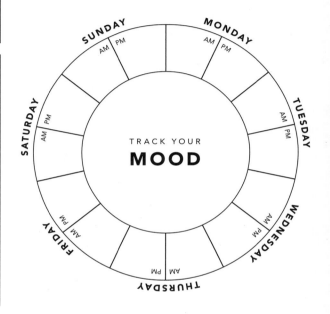

OCTOBER 2023

Mo	Tu	We	Th	Fr	Sa	Su
						1
2	3	4	5	6	7	8
9	10	11	12	13	14	15
16	17	18	19	20	21	22
23	24	25	26	27	28	29
30	31					

DECEMBER 2023

Mo	Tu	We	Th	Fr	Sa	Su
				1	2	3
4	5	6	7	8	9	10
11	12	13	14	15	16	17
18	19	20	21	22	23	24
25	26	27	28	29	30	31

(COLOR) SCALE

NOTES

30 | **MONDAY**

31 | **TUESDAY**   *Halloween*

1 | **WEDNESDAY**

2 | **THURSDAY**

3 | **FRIDAY**

4 | **SATURDAY**

5 | **SUNDAY**   *Daylight Saving Time ends (USA, CAN)*

REFLECT ON YOUR MOODS THIS WEEK.

WHAT IMPACTED YOUR MOOD?

POSITIVE	NEUTRAL	NEGATIVE

CREATE A LIST OF AFFIRMATIONS TO TELL YOURSELF THIS WEEK. REMIND YOURSELF ABOUT THE QUALITIES YOU ADMIRE MOST ABOUT YOU.

THIS WEEK'S HAPPY MOMENT

THIS WEEK I'M GRATEFUL FOR

WEEKLY GOALS

1 _____

_____

2 _____

_____

3 _____

_____

Your task is not to seek for love, but merely to seek and find all the barriers within yourself that you have built against it.

—RUMI

TO DO

- • _____
- • _____
- • _____
- • _____
- • _____
- • _____
- • _____
- • _____
- • _____
- • _____

TRACK YOUR
MOOD

SUNDAY AM PM
MONDAY AM PM
TUESDAY AM PM
WEDNESDAY AM PM
THURSDAY AM PM
FRIDAY AM PM
SATURDAY AM PM

OCTOBER 2023

Mo	Tu	We	Th	Fr	Sa	Su
						1
2	3	4	5	6	7	8
9	10	11	12	13	14	15
16	17	18	19	20	21	22
23	24	25	26	27	28	29
30	31					

(COLOR) SCALE

DECEMBER 2023

Mo	Tu	We	Th	Fr	Sa	Su
				1	2	3
4	5	6	7	8	9	10
11	12	13	14	15	16	17
18	19	20	21	22	23	24
25	26	27	28	29	30	31

NOTES

NOVEMBER

6 | **MONDAY**

7 | **TUESDAY** *Election Day*

8 | **WEDNESDAY**

9 | **THURSDAY**

10 | **FRIDAY**

11 | **SATURDAY** *Veterans Day (USA)*
Remembrance Day (CAN, UK)

12 | **SUNDAY** *Diwali begins*

REFLECT ON YOUR MOODS THIS WEEK.

WHAT IMPACTED YOUR MOOD?

POSITIVE	NEUTRAL	NEGATIVE

WRITE ABOUT A POSITIVE EXPERIENCE YOU HAD THIS WEEK. MAKE A POINT TO CELEBRATE ANY OF YOUR SUCCESSES, NO MATTER HOW SMALL OR LARGE.

THIS WEEK'S HAPPY MOMENT

THIS WEEK I'M GRATEFUL FOR

WEEKLY GOALS

1 --
----

2 --
----

3 --

TO DO

- --
- --
- --
- --
- --
- --
- --
- --
- --

Our feelings are our most genuine paths to knowledge.

—AUDRE LORDE

TRACK YOUR
MOOD

SUNDAY AM PM · MONDAY AM PM · TUESDAY AM PM · WEDNESDAY AM PM · THURSDAY AM PM · FRIDAY AM PM · SATURDAY AM PM

OCTOBER 2023

Mo	Tu	We	Th	Fr	Sa	Su
						1
2	3	4	5	6	7	8
9	10	11	12	13	14	15
16	17	18	19	20	21	22
23	24	25	26	27	28	29
30	31					

(COLOR) SCALE

DECEMBER 2023

Mo	Tu	We	Th	Fr	Sa	Su
				1	2	3
4	5	6	7	8	9	10
11	12	13	14	15	16	17
18	19	20	21	22	23	24
25	26	27	28	29	30	31

NOTES

NOVEMBER

13 MONDAY

14 TUESDAY

15 WEDNESDAY

16 THURSDAY

17 FRIDAY

18 SATURDAY

19 SUNDAY

REFLECT ON YOUR MOODS THIS WEEK.

WHAT IMPACTED YOUR MOOD?

POSITIVE	NEUTRAL	NEGATIVE

WHAT ARE THREE WAYS YOU CAN IMPROVE YOUR MOOD THIS COMING
WEEK?

THIS WEEK'S HAPPY MOMENT

THIS WEEK I'M GRATEFUL FOR

WEEKLY GOALS

1

2

3

TO DO

- --
- --
- --
- --
- --
- --
- --
- --
- --
- --

> Though I am often in the depths of misery, there is still calmness, pure harmony, and music inside me.
>
> —VINCENT VAN GOGH

TRACK YOUR MOOD

SUNDAY AM PM · MONDAY AM PM · TUESDAY AM PM · WEDNESDAY AM PM · THURSDAY AM PM · FRIDAY AM PM · SATURDAY AM PM

OCTOBER 2023

Mo	Tu	We	Th	Fr	Sa	Su
						1
2	3	4	5	6	7	8
9	10	11	12	13	14	15
16	17	18	19	20	21	22
23	24	25	26	27	28	29
30	31					

DECEMBER 2023

Mo	Tu	We	Th	Fr	Sa	Su
				1	2	3
4	5	6	7	8	9	10
11	12	13	14	15	16	17
18	19	20	21	22	23	24
25	26	27	28	29	30	31

(COLOR) SCALE

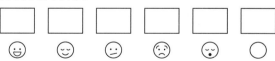

NOTES

NOVEMBER

20 MONDAY

21 TUESDAY

22 WEDNESDAY

23 THURSDAY · *Thanksgiving Day*

24 FRIDAY

25 SATURDAY

26 SUNDAY

REFLECT ON YOUR MOODS THIS WEEK.

WHAT IMPACTED YOUR MOOD?

POSITIVE	NEUTRAL	NEGATIVE

SOMETIMES WE CAN BE CRUELER TO OURSELVES THAN WE DESERVE. WHAT IS YOUR CURRENT RELATIONSHIP WITH YOURSELF? IS IT POSITIVE OR SOMETHING YOU COULD IMPROVE?

THIS WEEK'S HAPPY MOMENT

THIS WEEK I'M GRATEFUL FOR

WEEKLY GOALS

1 ----------------------------------
----

2 ----------------------------------
----

3 ----------------------------------

Each man must look to himself to teach him the meaning of life. It is not something discovered: it is something molded.

—ANTOINE DE SAINT EXUPÉRY

TO DO

• ----------------------------------
• ----------------------------------
• ----------------------------------
• ----------------------------------
• ----------------------------------
• ----------------------------------
• ----------------------------------
• ----------------------------------
• ----------------------------------
• ----------------------------------

TRACK YOUR
MOOD

SUNDAY · AM | PM · MONDAY · AM | PM · TUESDAY · AM | PM · WEDNESDAY · AM | PM · THURSDAY · AM | PM · FRIDAY · AM | PM · SATURDAY · AM | PM

OCTOBER 2023

Mo	Tu	We	Th	Fr	Sa	Su
						1
2	3	4	5	6	7	8
9	10	11	12	13	14	15
16	17	18	19	20	21	22
23	24	25	26	27	28	29
30	31					

DECEMBER 2023

Mo	Tu	We	Th	Fr	Sa	Su
				1	2	3
4	5	6	7	8	9	10
11	12	13	14	15	16	17
18	19	20	21	22	23	24
25	26	27	28	29	30	31

(COLOR) SCALE

NOTES

27 MONDAY

28 TUESDAY

29 WEDNESDAY

30 THURSDAY *St. Andrew's Day (SCT)*

1 FRIDAY

2 SATURDAY

3 SUNDAY

REFLECT ON YOUR MOODS THIS WEEK.

WHAT IMPACTED YOUR MOOD?

POSITIVE	NEUTRAL	NEGATIVE

MONTHLY REFLECTION: WHAT MOST AFFECTED YOUR MOOD THIS MONTH?

THIS WEEK'S HAPPY MOMENT

THIS WEEK I'M GRATEFUL FOR

DECEMBER

	MONDAY	TUESDAY	WEDNESDAY	THURSDAY	FRIDAY
49					1
50	4	5	6	7 *Hanukkah begins; Pearl Harbor Day*	8
51	11	12	13	14	15
52	18	19	20	21 *Winter begins (Northern Hemisphere)*	22
53	25 *Christmas Day*	26 *Kwanzaa begins; Boxing Day (AUS, CAN, NZ, UK)*	27	28	29

SATURDAY	SUNDAY
2	3
9	10
16	17
23	24
	Christmas Eve
30	31
	New Year's Eve

49
50
51
52
53

NOTES

MONTHLY GOAL TRACKER

GOAL:
----

① ② ③ ④ ⑤ ⑥ ⑦ ⑧ ⑨ ⑩ ⑪ ⑫ ⑬ ⑭
⑮ ⑯ ⑰ ⑱ ⑲ ⑳ 21 22 23 24 25 26 27 28
29 30 31

GOAL:
----

① ② ③ ④ ⑤ ⑥ ⑦ ⑧ ⑨ ⑩ ⑪ ⑫ ⑬ ⑭
⑮ ⑯ ⑰ ⑱ ⑲ ⑳ 21 22 23 24 25 26 27 28
29 30 31

GOAL:
----

① ② ③ ④ ⑤ ⑥ ⑦ ⑧ ⑨ ⑩ ⑪ ⑫ ⑬ ⑭
⑮ ⑯ ⑰ ⑱ ⑲ ⑳ 21 22 23 24 25 26 27 28
29 30 31

WEEKLY GOALS

1

2

3

TO DO

- -----------------------------------
- -----------------------------------
- -----------------------------------
- -----------------------------------
- -----------------------------------
- -----------------------------------
- -----------------------------------
- -----------------------------------
- -----------------------------------
- -----------------------------------

Our feelings are not there to be cast out or conquered. They're there to be engaged and expressed with imagination and intelligence.

—T. K. COLEMAN

TRACK YOUR
MOOD

SUNDAY · MONDAY · TUESDAY · WEDNESDAY · THURSDAY · FRIDAY · SATURDAY (AM / PM)

NOVEMBER 2023

Mo	Tu	We	Th	Fr	Sa	Su
		1	2	3	4	5
6	7	8	9	10	11	12
13	14	15	16	17	18	19
20	21	22	23	24	25	26
27	28	29	30			

(COLOR) SCALE

☺ ☺ 😐 ☹ 😴 ◯

JANUARY 2024

Mo	Tu	We	Th	Fr	Sa	Su
1	2	3	4	5	6	7
8	9	10	11	12	13	14
15	16	17	18	19	20	21
22	23	24	25	26	27	28
29	30	31				

NOTES

DECEMBER

4 | MONDAY

5 | TUESDAY

6 | WEDNESDAY

7 | THURSDAY *Hanukkah begins*
Pearl Harbor Day

8 | FRIDAY

9 | SATURDAY

10 | SUNDAY

REFLECT ON YOUR MOODS THIS WEEK.

WHAT IMPACTED YOUR MOOD?

POSITIVE	NEUTRAL	NEGATIVE

WRITE DOWN THE TASKS YOU WANT TO ACCOMPLISH THIS WEEK. MAKE SURE TO INCLUDE SOME TIME FOR RELAXING.

THIS WEEK'S HAPPY MOMENT

THIS WEEK I'M GRATEFUL FOR

WEEKLY GOALS

1

2

3

TO DO

- • ---------------------------------
- • ---------------------------------
- • ---------------------------------
- • ---------------------------------
- • ---------------------------------
- • ---------------------------------
- • ---------------------------------
- • ---------------------------------
- • ---------------------------------
- • ---------------------------------

Our successes and failures come and go—they neither define us not do they determine our worthiness.

—KRISTIN NEFF

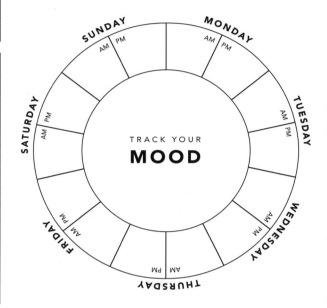

NOVEMBER 2023

Mo	Tu	We	Th	Fr	Sa	Su
		1	2	3	4	5
6	7	8	9	10	11	12
13	14	15	16	17	18	19
20	21	22	23	24	25	26
27	28	29	30			

JANUARY 2024

Mo	Tu	We	Th	Fr	Sa	Su
1	2	3	4	5	6	7
8	9	10	11	12	13	14
15	16	17	18	19	20	21
22	23	24	25	26	27	28
29	30	31				

(COLOR) SCALE

NOTES

DECEMBER

11 | **MONDAY**

12 | **TUESDAY**

13 | **WEDNESDAY**

14 | **THURSDAY**

15 | **FRIDAY**

16 | **SATURDAY**

17 | **SUNDAY**

REFLECT ON YOUR MOODS THIS WEEK.

WHAT IMPACTED YOUR MOOD?

POSITIVE	NEUTRAL	NEGATIVE

WHAT WAS THE BEST DECISION YOU EVER MADE? WHAT MADE IT SO GREAT?

THIS WEEK'S HAPPY MOMENT

THIS WEEK I'M GRATEFUL FOR

WEEKLY GOALS

1 ....
....

2 ....
....

3 ....
....
....

TO DO

- ....
- ....
- ....
- ....
- ....
- ....
- ....
- ....
- ....
- ....

Joy & Woe are woven fine/ A Clothing for the soul divine / Under every grief & pine / Runs a joy with silken twine.

—WILLIAM BLAKE, "AUGURIES OF INNOCENCE"

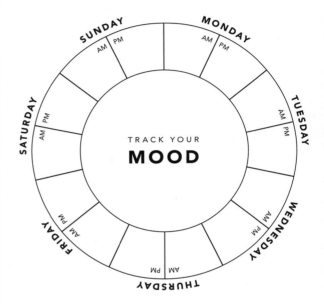

TRACK YOUR
MOOD

NOVEMBER 2023

Mo	Tu	We	Th	Fr	Sa	Su
		1	2	3	4	5
6	7	8	9	10	11	12
13	14	15	16	17	18	19
20	21	22	23	24	25	26
27	28	29	30			

JANUARY 2024

Mo	Tu	We	Th	Fr	Sa	Su
1	2	3	4	5	6	7
8	9	10	11	12	13	14
15	16	17	18	19	20	21
22	23	24	25	26	27	28
29	30	31				

(COLOR) SCALE

NOTES

DECEMBER

18 | MONDAY

19 | TUESDAY

20 | WEDNESDAY

21 | THURSDAY   *Winter begins (Northern Hemisphere)*

22 | FRIDAY

23 | SATURDAY

24 | SUNDAY   *Christmas Eve*

REFLECT ON YOUR MOODS THIS WEEK.

WHAT IMPACTED YOUR MOOD?

POSITIVE	NEUTRAL	NEGATIVE

WHAT ADVICE WOULD YOU HAVE WANTED TO HEAR AT THE BEGINNING
OF THIS YEAR ON YOUR MOOD JOURNEY? IS THERE ANY ADVICE YOU
WANT TO TELL YOURSELF AS YOU GO INTO THE NEW YEAR?

THIS WEEK'S HAPPY MOMENT

THIS WEEK I'M GRATEFUL FOR

WEEKLY GOALS

1

2

3

TO DO

- -------------------------------------
- -------------------------------------
- -------------------------------------
- -------------------------------------
- -------------------------------------
- -------------------------------------
- -------------------------------------
- -------------------------------------

Nothing in life is to be feared. It is only to be understood.

—MARIE CURIE

TRACK YOUR
MOOD

SUNDAY AM PM · MONDAY AM PM · TUESDAY AM PM · WEDNESDAY AM PM · THURSDAY AM PM · FRIDAY AM PM · SATURDAY AM PM

NOVEMBER 2023

Mo	Tu	We	Th	Fr	Sa	Su
		1	2	3	4	5
6	7	8	9	10	11	12
13	14	15	16	17	18	19
20	21	22	23	24	25	26
27	28	29	30			

JANUARY 2024

Mo	Tu	We	Th	Fr	Sa	Su
1	2	3	4	5	6	7
8	9	10	11	12	13	14
15	16	17	18	19	20	21
22	23	24	25	26	27	28
29	30	31				

(COLOR) SCALE

NOTES

DECEMBER

25 | **MONDAY**   *Christmas Day*

26 | **TUESDAY**   *Kwanzaa begins*
Boxing Day (AUS, CAN, NZ, UK)

27 | **WEDNESDAY**

28 | **THURSDAY**

29 | **FRIDAY**

30 | **SATURDAY**

31 | **SUNDAY**   *New Year's Eve*

REFLECT ON YOUR MOODS THIS WEEK.

WHAT IMPACTED YOUR MOOD?

POSITIVE	NEUTRAL	NEGATIVE

YEAR IN REFLECTION: LIST SOME WAYS YOU'VE GROWN SINCE THE BEGINNING OF THE YEAR.

THIS WEEK'S HAPPY MOMENT

THIS WEEK I'M GRATEFUL FOR

YOUR YEAR IN REVIEW

LOG YOUR DAILY MOODS

Dates	Week	Mo	Tu	We	Th	Fr	Sa	Su	Dates	Week	Mo	Tu	We	Th	Fr	Sa	Su
12/26-1/1	01								6/26-7/2	27							
1/2-1/8	02								7/3-7/9	28							
1/9-1/15	03								7/10-7/16	29							
1/16-1/22	04								7/17-7/23	30							
1/23-1/29	05								7/24-7/30	31							
1/30-2/5	06								7/31-8/6	32							
2/6-2/12	07								8/7-8/13	33							
2/13-2/19	08								8/14-8/20	34							
2/20-2/26	09								8/21-8/27	35							
2/27-3/5	10								8/28-9/3	36							
3/6-3/12	11								9/4-9/10	37							
3/13-3/19	12								9/11-9/17	38							
3/20-3/26	13								9/18-9/24	39							
3/27-4/2	14								9/25-10/1	40							
4/3-4/9	15								10/2-10/8	41							
4/10-4/16	16								10/9-10/15	42							
4/17-4/23	17								10/16-10/22	43							
4/24-4/30	18								10/23-10/29	44							
5/1-5/7	19								10/30-11/5	45							
5/8-5/14	20								11/6-11/12	46							
5/15-5/21	21								11/13-11/19	47							
5/22-5/28	22								11/20-11/26	48							
5/29-6/4	23								11/27-12/3	49							
6/5-6/11	24								12/4-12/10	50							
6/12-6/18	25								12/11-12/17	51							
6/19-6/25	26								12/18-12/24	52							
									12/25-12/31	53							

(COLOR) SCALE

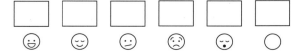